Conversations on the Future of Mission

First Fruits Press
The Academic Open Press of Asbury Theological Seminary
204 N. Lexington Ave., Wilmore, KY 40390
859-858-2236
first.fruits@asburyseminary.edu
asbury.to/firstfruits

Working Papers of the American Society of Missiology

ASM

American Society of Missiology

Edited by

Robert A. Danielson

William L. Selvidge

First Fruits Press
The Academic Open Press of Asbury Theological Seminary
204 N. Lexington Ave., Wilmore, KY 40390
859-858-2236
first.fruits@asburyseminary.edu
asbury.to/firstfruits

Conversations on the Future of Mission
Edited by Robert A. Danielson and William L. Selvidge

First Fruits Press, ©2018
Digital version at http://place.asburyseminary.edu/academicbooks/16/

ISBN: 9781621717676 (print), 9781621717683 (digital), 9781621717690 (kindle)

First Fruits Press
B.L. Fisher Library
Asbury Theological Seminary
204 N. Lexington Ave.
Wilmore, KY 40390
http://place.asburyseminary.edu/firstfruits

American Society of Missiology (2016 : Wheaton, Illinois)
Conversations on the Future of Mission / American Society of Missiology; edited by Robert A.
Danielson, William L. Selvidge. -- Wilmore, Kentucky: First Fruits Press, ©2018.
      xiv, 111 pages : illustrations; 21 cm. – (Working Papers of the American Society of
      Missiology; Volume V)
      Includes bibliographical references
      ISBN - 13: 9781621717676 (pbk.)
      1. Missions--Theory--Congresses. 2. Christianity and culture--Congresses. 3.
      Communication--Religious aspects--Christianity--Congresses. I. Title. II. Danielson,
      Robert A. (Robert Alden), 1969- III. Selvidge, William L..
BV2000.W674 Vol. 5

Cover design by Jon Ramsay

Table of Contents

Introduction

ROBERT DANIELSON

In 2017 the American Society of Missiology addressed a number of topics related to the Future of Mission. In this volume of the Working Papers of The American Society of Missiology (volume five in the series) we have organized the submitted papers to be part of a conversation about this topic. Where is missiology headed in the future? How has our current context shaped how mission is done and where it will be headed? These are important issues for our profession, and while we do not have all the answers to what the future holds, we can begin to see some suggestions that might give us hints to prepare for more changes to come.

Globalization and its impact is one important aspect influencing the future of missions. In the first article in this volume, David W. Scott examines how globalization has impacted the United Methodist Church Global Ministries as it has adopted the popular slogan, "From Everywhere to Everywhere." Just by changing the missional vision and goals of the organization to meet this globalized reality, we can begin to influence how mission is perceived and worked out at the institutional level. This is followed by an in depth look at the Onnuri Community Church by missiologist, J. Nelson Jennings. This case study examines globalization in mission by looking at Korean views of mission within a specific congregational setting. As the Church becomes more globalized we can expect greater influence in the field of missiology from non-western sources. How ready are we for this reality, and where can we begin to look to see how the future of mission will develop in these areas? Case studies, such as Jennings' work, provide a good start for answering such questions.

Joyce del Rosario raises another important and necessary trend in the future of missiology. There is a growing need for missiologists and mission practitioners to come together and work as partners to solve growing problems in our world. By looking at her work on both sides of this divide, especially in her work with the Christian Community Development Association, del Rosario points out how practitioners have little time for academic and theological reflection on their experiences, while academics frequently do not understand the realities of mission on the ground because of the time they must invest is research and writing. For the effective work of future mission endeavors it is vital that these two groups come together and find new ways to help each other.

Finally, for the first time, the Working Papers series has tried to capture the vitality of a panel presentation, which focused on a course entitled "Mission in Context." This course was part of a unique partnership between Louisville Presbyterian Theological Seminary and Seminario Evangelico de Teologia in Cuba. Bringing students and faculty together to learn from each other about the religious context and the impact of mission is an exciting example of missional partnerships that shows the way for greater educational opportunities in the future. Clifton Kirkpatrick, Ofelia Ortega, and Juan J. Sarmiento each demonstrate in their own way how this innovative type of learning can be applied. Joint educational projects like this are an important part of developing a missiology for the future.

In this work, we are in the third year of a new endeavor of the American Society of Missiology. During annual meetings, many professionals, practitioners, and students present informative papers in a variety of different areas. Often these papers are works in progress, not quite ready for publication, or are ideas looking for professional feedback. Sometimes these papers are just areas expressing the many side interests of the presenters. In most of these cases, these works will not be published as formal articles in *Missiology* or other academic journals, but they still represent excellent ideas and works in progress that can stimulate the missiological community. To keep these ideas alive and active, the ASM decided to launch a series of volumes entitled "working papers." These papers have been presented at the annual meeting and the authors have polished them based on feedback received at the annual meeting, however these papers have not been peer-reviewed and should still be read in that light. They represent current ongoing academic thinking by current and rising missiologists and are presented here to encourage ongoing academic debate and critical thinking in the field of missiology.

From Everywhere to Everywhere

Assessing the Practice of a Denominational Mission Slogan

DAVID W. SCOTT
UMC GLOBAL MINISTRIES

DOI: 10.7252/Paper. 000074

Abstract

This paper explores the uses of the phrase "from everywhere to everywhere" as an unofficial motto by The United Methodist Church's General Board of Global Ministries. It first surveys the usage of the term in the broader Christian context. It then examines ways in which the motto's usage at Global Ministries recognizes changes but also remains aspirational in two areas: recruitment and deployment of mission personnel and finances and structures of mission agencies. It also notes that while the phrase is sometimes used in the broader context to refer to the United States as a mission field, this usage is not prominent at Global Ministries. The paper concludes that while mission agencies must necessarily be informed by wider missiological trends, their finite nature will make them limited in their ability to fully implement these trends.

The General Board of Global Ministries of The United Methodist Church has adopted the phrase "from everywhere to everywhere" as a motto for its work. Initially used to describe missionaries sent by Global Ministries, the phrase is now used by Global Ministries and others in The United Methodist Church to describe mission generally. Examining the ways in which this motto has intersected with the work of Global Ministries provides an opportunity to assess the role of denominational mission societies within the breadth of Christian mission today. Such an examination leads to the conclusion that while specific denominational entities should be informed by wider trends in the understanding of Christian mission, they will necessarily be limited in their ability to fully live into these understandings by their histories, their structures, their stakeholders, and their finite nature.

Before continuing with my paper, a quick disclaimer is in order. Astute audience members will have noted that I myself am the Director of Mission Theology at Global Ministries. My remarks, however, should in no way be construed as representing the official views of Global Ministries. Instead, they are the personal analysis of an academic who has had the good fortune of serving as a participant-observer at the organization.

HISTORY OF A CATCHPHRASE

Global Ministries is not the only nor the first Christian entity or person to use the phrase "from everywhere to everywhere." Indeed, this phrase has become commonplace across many disparate parts of mission-oriented Christianity.[1] The earliest published use of the phrase that I have identified came in the title of a 1991 book by Bishop Michael Nazir-Ali.[2] Nazir-Ali's book had limited reception, though several other scholars did pick up on it and the phrase.[3]

---

1   I want to thank my colleague Elliott Wright for helping me track down recent references to the phrase in the Christian popular press.

2   Michael Nazir-Ali. *From Everywhere to Everywhere: A World View of Christian Witness*. (London: Flame, 1990). The book was reprinted by Wipf and Stock in 2009 with the slightly amended title *From Everywhere to Everywhere: A World View of Christian Mission*.

3   See, for instance, James E. Plueddemann, "Theological Implications of Globalizing Missions." In *Globalizing Theology: Belief and Practice in an Era of World Christianity*, ed. Craig Ott and Harold A. Netland. (Grand Rapids, MI: Baker Academic, 2006), 250; Titus Pressler, "Mission Is Ministry in the Dimension of Difference: A Definition for the Twenty-first Century." *International Bulletin of Missionary Research* 34 no. 4 (October 2010), 201.

Additionally, the phrase seems to have been either independently reinvented by others or used without awareness of its origins, such that it is not entirely clear what the background of any particular reference is. Additional significant sources for the phrase appear to be Samuel Escobar's related phrase "from everywhere to everyone," used in the title of his widely popular 2003 book,[4] and the use of the phrase by Dr. Michael Cassidy in an address to the 2010 Third Lausanne Congress of the Lausanne Movement in Cape Town, South Africa.[5] Since its use at Cape Town in 2010, the popularity of the phrase has increased, including its use as a chapter title by popular Christian historian Mark Noll, though Noll does not give a source for the phrase.[6]

Within all these various instances, the phrase is used in three different ways: first, to talk about missionaries being sent "from everywhere to everywhere," second to talk about mission generally "from everywhere to everywhere," and third, to emphasize that everywhere, including the West, is now a location for mission. While missionaries and mission are conceptually related, it is important to make the distinction between the first two meanings, as the two uses do have different connotations.

Global Ministries' Embrace of "From Everywhere to Everywhere"

The phrase "from everywhere to everywhere" became part of Global Ministries' lexicon in the spring of 2012 in the March/April edition of *New World Outlook* and in General Secretary Thomas Kemper's remarks to the spring board meeting of Global Ministries.[7] In its initial use, Kemper applied the phrase

4   Samuel Escobar, *The New Global Mission: The Gospel from Everywhere to Everyone.* (Downers Grove, IL: InterVarsity Press, 2003). Escobar himself cites Nazir-Ali on p. 18. Incidentally, Allen Yeh has reversed Escobar's formulation of the phrase in the title of his recent book, *Polycentric Missiology: Twenty First Century Mission from Everyone to Everywhere* (Downers Grove, IL: InterVarsity Press, 2016).

5   See Dion Forster, "Missionaries from everywhere to everywhere," Blog, Lausanne Movement, (October 25, 2010), https://www.lausanne.org/about/blog/missionaries-from-everywhere-to-everywhere, accessed May 15, 2017.

6   Mark Noll, *Protestantism: A Very Short Introduction* (Oxford; New York: Oxford University Press, 2011), Chapter 8.

7   Thomas Kemper, "Missionaries for the 21st Century," *New World Outlook* (March/April 2012), http://www.umcmission.org/Learn-About-Us/News-and-Stories/2012/March/Missionaries-for-the-21st-Century, accessed May 15, 2017; Melissa Hinnen, "United Methodist Leader Affirms Importance of a Global Agency to Engage in the Church's Global Mission," News and Stories, Global Ministries (March 20, 2012),

primarily to Global Ministries' missionaries. Although Kemper wrote "that mission and missionaries must come from everywhere and be sent everywhere," the primary emphasis both in this phrase and in his writings in general seems to be on missionaries as individuals rather than on mission broadly as an activity.[8] Its primary context was a newly developed world map showing lines linking Global Ministries missionaries' countries of origin and their countries of assignment.[9]

Yet within two years of the phrase's introduction to Global Ministries, its use began to shift from referring solely to missionaries to referring to mission in general. Debra Tyree, for instance, used the phrase in late 2013 to describe worship resources with a global consciousness.[10] Kemper himself was speaking about "mission from everywhere to everywhere" as opposed to "missionaries from everywhere to everywhere" by late 2015.[11] When Global Ministries announced its plan to create regional offices in 2016, Rev. Mande Muyombo wrote, "The theology of our regional structure is based on our sense of mission 'from everywhere to everywhere'."[12] Muyombo's use highlights the full evolution of the phrase within Global Ministries, as it is not only linked to mission rather than just missionaries, but the quotation

---

http://www.umcmission.org/Learn-About-Us/News-and-Stories/2012/March/United-Methodist-Leader-Affirms-Importance-of-a-Global-Agency-to-Engage-in-the-Church-s-Global-Mission, accessed May 15, 2017.

8   Kemper, "Missionaries for the 21st Century." See also Thomas Kemper, "A Reflection on Missionaries Around the World," News and Stories, Global Ministries (October 2013), http://www.umcmission.org/Learn-About-Us/News-and-Stories/2013/October/1017-A-Reflection-on-Missionaries-Around-the-World, accessed May 15, 2017.

9   For a copy of the map, see http://www.umcmission.org/Learn-About-Us/News-and-Stories/2012/March/United-Methodist-Leader-Affirms-Importance-of-a-Global-Agency-to-Engage-in-the-Church-s-Global-Mission, accessed May 15, 2017.

10   Debra Tyree, "Thanksgiving Season Worship: From Everywhere to Everywhere," Calendar, Global Ministries (November 2013), http://www.umcmission.org/Find-Resources/Calendar/Thanksgiving, accessed May 15, 2017; Debra Tyree, "In Prayer "With": From Everywhere to Everywhere at the Turn of the New Year," Calendar, Global Ministries (December 2013), http://www.umcmission.org/Find-Resources/Calendar/In-Prayer-With-From-Everywhere-to-Everywhere-at-the-Turn-of-the-New-Year, accessed May 15, 2017.

11   Thomas Kemper, "Extending the Global Mission Conversation," *New World Outlook* (November/December 2015), http://www.umcmission.org/Find-Resources/New-World-Outlook-Magazine/New-World-Outlook-Archives/2015/November/December/1103globalmissionconversation, accessed May 15, 2017.

12   Mande Muyombo, "No Center No Periphery: A Regional Approach to Mission," *New World Outlook* (July/August 2016), http://www.umcmission.org/find-resources/new-world-outlook-magazine/2016/july/august/0712noperiphery, accessed May 15, 2017.

marks indicate its use as a recognized motto or slogan within the agency. This newer use has not, however, eclipsed the original sense as applied to missionaries.[13]

MISSIONARIES FROM EVERYWHERE TO EVERYWHERE

Having established the history and meanings of this phrase, both outside and within Global Ministries, it is now time to assess why and to what end the phrase has been used. I will do so by examining both of the meanings with which it has been used by Global Ministries – its original use applied to missionaries and its broader use applied to mission in general – and its third meaning of the West as a mission field, which has not been a significant use in Global Ministries. I will deal with its application to missionaries first.

Like most American denominational mission societies, Global Ministries' past reflects traditional, Americentric concepts of mission and a traditional, American base of support. While Global Ministries and its predecessors has sponsored missionaries from a variety of nationalities for over a century, the vast majority of its missionaries have been Westerners, and the vast majority of those Westerners have been American. Nevertheless, in light of shifts in both the membership of The United Methodist Church and the composition of world Christianity as a whole, Global Ministries identified the need to alter some aspects of its historic model of operations.

In particular, Global Ministries recognized eight or nine years ago the importance of developing a missionary corps that reflected the diversity of national origins of United Methodist members and other Global Ministries partners. This was the context in which the phrase "from everywhere to everywhere" was introduced. It was intended to signify a shift in how Global Ministries thought about recruiting and deploying missionaries.

It is hard to assess how much impact this phrase has had. Already at the phrase's introduction, nearly 50% of new missionaries (including regular and young adult missionaries) sent by Global Ministries came from outside the United States.[14] In contrast, 41% of regular missionaries trained in spring 2017 but 68% of young adult

13   See, for instance, Joy Kitanga, "Global Mission Fellows: From Everywhere to Everywhere," News and Stories, Global Ministries (December 2016), http://www.umcmission.org/learn-about-us/news-and-stories/2016/december/1229global-mission-fellows-from-everywhere-to-everywhere, accessed May 15, 2017.

14   Hinnen, "United Methodist Leader."

missionaries trained in summer and fall 2016 were from outside the United States, for a combined total of 62% of new missionaries from outside the United States.[15]

While these data are clear, their significance is not. Why is there a difference between regular and young adult missionaries? Are these indicators of long-term trends or merely data points? 62% is greater than the percentage of United Methodist members outside the US, but since Global Ministries works with partners from other denominational traditions, what should be the goal? Whatever the goal, does this figure represent progress? If so, how much of it is attributable to use of the slogan? The answers to these and other questions are hard to say.

Two conclusions at least do, however, seem reasonable. First, the slogan reflects long-term shifts in missionary recruitment, whether or not it has had any short term causal role in these shifts. Two decades or more ago, the percentage of Global Ministries missionaries coming from outside the United States would have been nowhere near 50%. Thus, at very least, the use of the phrase applied to missionaries has helped crystalize an understanding of a process already underway.

Second, and perhaps not surprisingly, the use of the slogan has not resolved all issues around developing an international group of missionary personnel. One colleague asserted that the map intended to reflect the shift in missionaries to a "from everywhere to everywhere" model actually reflected on-going American dominance. Some host locations still prefer American missionaries because they are seen as having more access to American funds. All missionaries, regardless of their national origin, are asked to itinerate and raise funds in the United States. US Visas remain an issue for some missionary candidates, which can complicate training and prohibit some pairings of sending and receiving "everywheres." Certain categories of mission service are only open to those from the United States or those from outside the United States for a variety of historical, practical, and strategic reasons. Some current policies only recognize a single national origin for missionaries, though

15   "United Methodist Church to Send 45 New Young Adult Missionaries," News and Stories, Global Ministries (July 2016), http://www.umcmission.org/learn-about-us/news-and-stories/2016/july/0728newyoungadultmissionaries, accessed May 15, 2017; "Jesus Calls…Young United Methodist Missionaries Follow," News and Stories, Global Ministries (August 2016), http://www.umcmission.org/learn-about-us/news-and-stories/2016/august/0804jesuscalls, accessed May 15, 2017; Elliott Wright and Ivy Couch, "Seventeen New United Methodist Missionaries to be Blessed and Sent in Near Future," News and Stories, Global Ministries (May 2017), http://www.umcmission.org/learn-about-us/news-and-stories/2017/may/0502seventeen-new-united-methodist-missionaries-to-be-blessed-and-sent-in-near-future, accessed May 15, 2017.

some missionaries may be dual citizens.[16] Mission remains a complex endeavor, perhaps even more so in the wake of the shift in mission personnel.

MISSION FROM EVERYWHERE TO EVERYWHERE

I turn now from analyzing missionaries as from everywhere to everywhere to analyzing mission as from everywhere to everywhere. This shift raises the question of what is entailed in mission apart from missionaries. Certainly, one could give theological answers to this question – the Holy Spirit or the movement of God is involved. Yet, in terms of tangible, this-worldly components of mission beyond missionaries, two that stand out are resources and organizations. I will thus address both topics.

While Global Ministries has achieved some level of success in making changes in its pool of missionary personnel, its funding remains overwhelmingly American. United Methodists from the United States give the majority of support both through denominational funds (called the World Service Fund) and through direct gifts. Money is certainly not the only resource or asset involved in mission, but its ability to be translated into other resources makes it perhaps the most important. Moreover, Global Ministries has successfully sought to increase levels of mission self-support through programs such as the In Mission Together program and 50/50 Covenant Partnerships. Nevertheless, an overwhelming majority of the money that Global Ministries transfers from one country to another goes from the United States to elsewhere.

This arrangement arises from a confluence of factors. First is historic precedent in how denominational funds are collected and how gifts to Global Ministries are cultivated. Closely related to and intertwined with these patterns is an older notion of mission that sees mission as flowing from the US to the rest of the world. This understanding persists in many places in The United Methodist Church at large, limiting the extent to which Global Ministries can attempt to shift funding patterns. Nevertheless, the action by the UMC's recent General Conference to approve a plan to collect some denominational funds from outside the US represents a step forward. Moreover, a slogan such as "from everywhere to everywhere" has the potential to provoke further conversations about how resources (economic and otherwise) are shared in the UMC.

---

16   This point was made to me by a colleague in a personal email.

The second cause for the dominance of American money is the massive economic inequalities among nations in the current world system. A large part of the reason money flows from the United States to the Democratic Republic of Congo, for instance, and not the other way around, is that the DRC has a per capita GDP that is 1% that of the US. Money flows from the US because there is more money in the US than most other locations in the world. While Global Ministries works for economic justice, producing substantial, systemic changes to global economic inequalities is probably beyond the agency's ability.

Yet, even when United Methodists try to send money in the "reverse direction," it can be rebuffed because of persistent old understandings of mission. A colleague told me of a Zimbabwean United Methodist congregation that took up a collection to support a Swiss United Methodist congregation that was struggling to stay open. The Swiss refused the Zimbabweans' money, offending them in the process. Such an attitude goes against Global Ministries' emphasis on mutuality, but reflects the challenges of its ecclesial context.

The third reason that Global Ministries money flows from the United States is the existence of alternate United Methodist mission agencies in Europe, the location of the other financially well-to-do United Methodist units. The branches of The United Methodist Church in Germany, Switzerland, and Norway all have their own mission agencies, which serve as the primary conduit for money from these economically advanced nations to mission partners in less well-economically advanced countries.

This third point raises the question of whether mission agencies themselves can be "from everywhere to everywhere." Essentially, there are two sides to this debate. One argues that mission agencies can transcend their national origins to become truly global organizations that, while perhaps headquartered in a particular country, function through the contributions and ownership of supporters and staff from many countries, if not quite everywhere. This is the approach that Global Ministries is attempting to take.

One significant aspect of Global Ministries' efforts in this regard is the creation of regional offices around the world. As Muyombo explains, "These regional offices will provide valuable on-the-ground resources, enabling Global Ministries to be more fully present, regularly engaged, and quickly and easily responsive to the global church and its partners in key world regions." He continues, "[O]ur sense today is that there isn't a center anymore—that doing mission lies in mutuality, looking at each other as equal partners and learning from one another."[17] These regional offices in Asia, Latin America, and Africa will be staffed primarily by employees with roots in the area. Furthermore, Global Ministries' staff members in its Atlanta headquarters come from a wide variety of countries, though the majority are probably from the United States.[18]

There are certainly challenges to Global Ministries' attempt to become a mission agency that is from everywhere and not just an American agency. As mentioned, the headquarters is in the US, the majority of staff come from the US, the majority of current missionaries are from the US (even if the trend has been toward more missionaries from outside the US), and the significant majority of funding comes from the US. Large portions of the policies employed at the agency are taken from US corporate culture. At what point in the organization's development does it become a truly global organization and not just an American organization with global features? The answer is not clear.

Moreover, there are those who would argue that the goal for mission that goes from everywhere to everywhere is not to have mission agencies that send missionaries from everywhere but to have mission agencies everywhere that send missionaries. James Plueddemann, for instance, argues, "Mission agencies will need to expand their focus from evangelism and church planting to mission-agency planting. Mission agencies must change organizational structures so they can partner with the mission agencies that grow out of the churches they helped to plant."[19]

As noted, The United Methodist Church already has indigenous mission agencies in Germany, Switzerland, and Norway. An alternative approach to Global Ministries' current approach would be to facilitate the development of additional United Methodist mission agencies in the Philippines, DRC, Mozambique, Liberia, etc. I am not recommending that Global Ministries take such a strategy; I am only noting that such a strategy would also be consistent with mission "from everywhere

---

17   Muyombo, "No Center No Periphery."

18   "Who Makes Up Global Ministries' Staff?" *New World Outlook* (November/December 2015), http://www.umcmission.org/Find-Resources/New-World-Outlook-Magazine/New-World-Outlook-Archives/2015/November/December/1111globalministriesstaff, accessed May 15, 2017, found that 58% of staff responding to an internal survey were from the US. There has been substantial staff turnover since then, but my sense is that the figure is probably similar today.

19   Plueddemann, 264-5.

to everywhere." Hence, such a motto must still be interpreted, especially when it comes to how to structure organizations to support this type of mission.

FROM EVERYWHERE TO THE UNITED STATES?

One final meaning of the phrase "from everywhere to everywhere" shifts the emphasis from the *from* everywhere portion (which is the focus of the prior two meaning) to the *to* everywhere portion. In particular, it emphasizes that the West, historically the sending region for missionaries and mission, is now a receiving region for missionaries and mission. While this sense of the phrase has been present elsewhere in the missiological conversation, it has largely not been part of Global Ministries' and United Methodists' use of the phrase. The reasons are complex, with a variety of factors internal to The United Methodist Church at play.

First, Global Ministries does and has long done mission work in the United States. While recruiting significant numbers of missionaries from outside the US is a new development for Global Ministries, deploying missionaries within the US is not a new development. Hence, Global Ministries has used the phrase to highlight the former and not the latter. The majority of missionaries deployed in the US are from the US (not "everywhere"), but as previously noted, visa restrictions outside Global Ministries' control reinforce this pattern.

Second, like other American denominations, The United Methodist Church has historically had many organizations designed to carry out some portion of its mission within the United States, but only a mission agency to carry out mission outside the United States. Exacerbating this distinction between domestic and foreign programs are the distinctions between mission and evangelism and mission and social concerns. The United Methodist Church as a whole has not yet discerned what constitutes mission and what separates mission from other areas of endeavor apart from geographic boundaries. Such conversations are underway as part of efforts to shift the denomination into a more global mode, but questions about mission and geography remain outstanding. Moreover, even while leaders are engaging in such conversations, many United Methodists remain tied to older ways of understanding mission, as previously noted.

Third, many American United Methodists struggle with a sense of lost cultural place and have been hesitant to an embrace an understanding of the church's role in the United States that sees the US as primarily a mission field as opposed to "home territory." While Global Ministries has certainly supported efforts to encourage Americans to develop a more missional understanding of their own context, such efforts have not been a major area of focus for the agency.

It is not necessarily a problem or failure that Global Ministries has not much explored this third meaning of "from everywhere to everywhere." Certainly, agencies can use their discretion to set their priorities and use language in one way and not another. It will be interesting to see, however, whether this third sense of the phrase will become more important at some later point in the organization's development.

CONCLUSION

I hope this exploration of Global Ministries' use of the phrase "from everywhere to everywhere" has accomplished several things. First, I hope it has provided a good examination of the possible meanings inherent in this phrase, which has become prominent not only in United Methodist circles but in mission circles broadly. Second, I hope it has highlighted the ways in which history, context, and structure all affect the ways in which a particular organization can live out this (or any other) mission slogan. Third and finally, I hope it has affirmed that mission in its totality is far beyond the ability of any one organization, no matter how well-run, to reflect in its practices. Mission is ultimately God's mission, or the *missio Dei*, and God requires the sincere, faithful, and earnest efforts of all Christians from everywhere through all organizational channels to participate in that mission to everywhere.

Missional Missions

A Missiological Case Study of Onnuri Community Church

Rev. J. Nelson Jennings, PhD

Onnuri Community Church – Mission Pastor and Consultant, International Liaison

DOI: 10.7252/Paper. 000075

Abstract:

This is a case study about Onnuri Community Church (OCC), one of the megachurches based in Seoul. Composed for presentation at the June 2017 annual meeting of the American Society of Missiology, the study embraces the importance of interaction between mission practice and missiological scholarship. As such, this study examines ongoing OCC efforts to integrate its extensive mission programs with missiological understandings, especially understandings of missional church ministry. OCC has recently entered both its fourth decade of history and its second generation of leadership. During this crucial transitional period, how OCC's mission practices and missiological understandings continue to interface will prove to be vital for its ongoing gospel ministries, both in the Seoul area and among peoples in many other parts of the world.

God's work has been palpable in the founding, development, and ministries of Onnuri Community Church (OCC). As a missiologist who now participates in OCC's life and mission, I will claim as well that OCC is perhaps the most mission-oriented church that I know.[1] That "mission-oriented" character includes all sorts of international initiatives, including what some would call a "traditional" sending of "overseas missionaries" and a bevy of newer initiatives, including a satellite TV network,[2] active NGO,[3] training of other Asian church leaders, and others. OCC's mission orientation also includes what more recently has been labeled "missional" emphases, namely holistic ministries among peoples and communities in OCC's immediate vicinity in Seoul, as well as in other parts of South Korea and internationally. Moreover, OCC's mission orientation is not simply one among several church programs, but it is closely intertwined with OCC's very nature and vision as a church. All of these factors and more lie behind this study's primary title, "Missional Missions."

OCC's vibrant mission orientation raises a variety of missiological questions needing the combined attention of practitioners and scholars. While there are hazards involved with an expatriate structuring an English-language analysis of any Korean entity like OCC, I have determined six such questions to guide this particular study. I have divided the questions into two sections labeled "Setting" and "Challenges":

A.   SETTING

- How has OCC's historical context shaped its mission orientation?

- What are some particular features that distinguish OCC's mission orientation?

- What does OCC's Korean character mean for its mission orientation?

---

1   Furthermore, starting with Sr. Pastor Lee Jae-hoon, OCC's mission leaders are genuinely open to critique, input, and suggestions for growth and improvement. That openness has helped tremendously my work as OCC Mission Consultant, a role I have been privileged to play since September 2015.

2   CGNTV, or "Christian Global Network." See the network's website at http://www.cgntv.net/. This and all other websites referenced in this paper were accessed on June 27, 2017.

3   "Better World." See their website at http://www.abetterworld.or.kr/.

B.   CHALLENGES

- What opposition has OCC faced in its mission orientation and emphases?

- Can OCC actually be a "missional megachurch," an oxymoron in some analyst's views?

- Can OCC integrate a "missional" orientation with a "traditional" missions approach?

These representative questions alone demand more analysis than a relatively brief study like this one can adequately offer. Through examining OCC's history along with relevant input from practitioners and scholars alike, despite my obvious limitations as a non-Korean[4] I hope at least to provide an entryway into appreciating the significance of both OCC's mission orientation and the related missiological questions that need ongoing consideration.[5]

A. SETTING

As outlined above, the first part of this case study about OCC looks at its overall setting, namely history, some distinctive mission traits, and OCC's Korean character.

---

4   Due to our family having lived as missionaries in Japan over a 13-year period, as well as having conducted PhD research largely in Japanese on Takakura Tokutaro (1885-1934), I have acquired Japanese traits and language that help in understanding Korea, Koreans, and Korean language (due to shared borrowings from Chinese). However, despite recently having lived in Korea for one year and currently making frequent multi-week visits there, and despite the warm and open embrace of OCC friends and colleagues, my Korean language ability is extremely limited, and hence Korean cultural sensibilities and written sources are still quite opaque to me. I should add that being a non-Korean does provide the advantage of an outsider's etic point of view. Moreover, as an experienced U.S.-American mission practitioner I have personal affinities with some of the issues that affect Korean missions that will emerge in this study.

5   While also involved with engaging this study's type of missiological questions, OCC's mission leaders are urgently focused on achieving more practical mission goals of evangelism, church-planting, leadership training, and holistic ministry. While considering how OCC might best achieve such practical goals is not the main subject of this study, such goals will inform the missiological discussions taking place here.

OCC's Historical Context

The history of OCC is part of Korean Christian history; similarly, Korean Christian history is part of worldwide Christian history.[6] As such, a comprehensive appreciation of Korean Christianity understands it in a more multifaceted manner than simply as the fruit of Western (U.S.-American) mission activity.[7] Most especially, God's fundamental role in bringing the Christian gospel to Koreans, on top of his having already been at work among contemporary Koreans' ancestors, is an essential component of a more full-orbed understanding of Korean Christian history. Stated differently, more than an example of Koreans embracing Christianity because U.S.-American missionaries came to Korea, OCC's history is one of myriad testimonies of how God has been restoring wayward people throughout the earth by bringing the good news of Jesus Christ to us, then maturing and using us to participate with him as part of that same ongoing mission.

In addition, the wider scope of avenues through which God has birthed and nurtured Christian belief among Korean people is partially blinded by largely bounded-set Korean Christian traditions,[8] including the generally Protestant traditions of life and scholarship among which OCC has developed.[9] For the sake

---

6   Thankfully there are scholarly accounts of Korean Christian history that take such a wider historical approach, e.g., Sebastian C. H. Kim and Kirsteen Kim, *A History of Korean Christianity*. New York: Cambridge University Press, 2014, Sung-Deuk Oak, *The Making of Korean Christianity: Protestant Encounters with Korean Religions, 1876-1915*. Studies in World Christianity Series, ed., Joel A. Carpenter. Waco, TX: Baylor University Press, 2013.

7   Anecdotally, I have often heard Korean Protestant Christian leaders explain the historical background of Korean Christianity by noting the Korean Church's indebtedness to the U.S.-American missionaries who brought the Christian gospel to Korea. One can see this emphasis in OCC founding pastor Ha Yong-jo and in OCC's ongoing historical understanding. See, for example, Pastor Ha's various comments in "South Korean Missionaries," a nine-minute public broadcasting documentary aired on August 10, 2007 and available online (both by video and script) at http://www.pbs.org/wnet/religionandethics/2007/08/10/august-10-2007-south-korean-missionaries/15711/.

8   As Kim and Kim note in their Introduction, "By writing about Korean Christianity as a whole we hope to overcome denominational divides that have blighted historiography. The most obvious challenge here is that there appears to be not one but two Christian histories in Korea: Catholic and Protestant." Kim and Kim, 3.

9   OCC's CGNTV recently produced a series of 34 moving, high-quality three-minute video clips about historical Korean Christians entitled "Fools for Christ in Korean Church History," available online at http://www.cgntv.net/tv/15200/1603/3344/vlist.cgn. The title reinforced OCC's overall vision phrase, "Fools for Christ" (announced by current Sr. Pastor Lee Jae-hoon as an amplification of the "Acts 29" vision articulated by the late Pastor Ha). During the latter half of my one year in Seoul (September 2015 – August 2016),

of cultivating a broader and more theocentric understanding of Korean Christianity as sketched above, non-Catholic Korean Christian believers and scholars (as well as non-Korean mission scholars) could manifest fuller understandings of Korean Christian beginnings in Japan in the 1590s,[10] the two-way Chinese-Korean connections through which Christian faith began to take further root among Koreans in the seventeenth and eighteenth centuries, then the thousands of Korean Christian-Catholic martyrdoms in the nineteenth century. Similarly, while there are notable exceptions,[11] much of Korean Catholic understanding and scholarship could stand to move beyond proceeding "as if Catholicism is the only form of Christianity to be found in Korea."[12] All forms of Korean Christianity have developed within the same overall Korean context, as well as within the varied contexts of the worldwide Korean diaspora. A robust theological and missiological viewpoint will look beyond blinders of denominational traditions, national frameworks, and encased religious explanations to see more clearly God's initiatives and corresponding Korean responses.

Understanding OCC and its mission orientation within that wider Korean and worldwide Christian history sheds extensive light on how OCC has developed in the ways that it has. On the one hand and for example, the central and foundational role for OCC played by its founding pastor, the late Rev. Ha Yong-

---

the clips would be shown in the sanctuary just prior to Sunday worship services. The series began with Pastor Gil Seon-ju, a prominent leader in the 1907 Pyongyang Revival; most all of the people featured in the series served in some relation to the Japanese Occupation and/or Korean War; and, all of them were Protestants. On a different note, the need for a wider awareness of historical avenues of Christian witness (vis-à-vis Korea and otherwise) is particularly true for an ahistorical viewpoint that focuses exclusively on God's work and people's individual relationships with God, apart from historical background or context.

10   James Huntley Grayson, "A Quarter-Millennium of Christianity in Korea," Ch. 1 in Robert E. Buswell and Timothy S. Lee, *Christianity in Korea*. University of Hawaii Press, 2006, 8-9. In addition, Lee Young-hoon, Sr. Pastor of Yoido Full Gospel Church, mentions some scholars who suggest much earlier Nestorian and then Catholic missionary contact with Koreans. Young-hoon Lee, *The Holy Spirit Movement in Korea: Its Historical and Theological Development*. Regnum Studies in Mission Series, eds., Julie C. Ma et al. Oxford: Regnum Books International, 2009, 19.

11   One example of a historical account of Korean Catholicism that occasionally mentions Korean Protestantism (albeit in largely parallel and self-acknowledged historically competitive fashion) is the online 16-part series by the Catholic Bishops' Conference of Korea, available at http://english.cbck.or.kr/history/.

12   Kim and Kim, 3.

Jo[13] (1946-2011), is beyond dispute. Indeed, the *raison d'être* of OCC's mid-1980s birth and ensuing mission is perhaps most fully and concisely articulated in Pastor Ha's late-in-life book, *Envisioning an Apostolic Church: Onnuri's Church Theory and Pastor Philosophy*.[14] At the same time, God's work in and through Ha Yong-jo's moving life experience, theological development, and spiritual emphases cannot be adequately understood or appreciated apart from considering wider Korean and worldwide Christian history.[15] Here I will limit the discussion to four salient historical matters and their connections with OCC.

Suffering

Korean Christianity has suffered martyrdoms from its earliest stages, including among slaves taken to Japan in the 1590s and during the establishment of the Catholic Church in Korea in the late eighteenth and then nineteenth centuries.[16] Wartime conditions and deprivation were part of the late nineteenth and early twentieth centuries in Korea, when the 1894-1895 Sino-Japan War and 1904-1905 Russo-Japan War raged as part of imperial clashes over East Asian territories, including the Korean Peninsula. The 1910-1945 Japanese colonization of Korea, with associated abuses of women and forced laborers, remains an unhealed and deep psychological and political wound for the Korean citizenry and government. The poverty, killing, and displacement during the 1950-1953 Korean War and its aftermath affected all Koreans alive prior to the current 40-and-under generation.

It was amidst such suffering from poverty and war that significant Christian growth occurred at different periods of Korea's volatile twentieth century.

---

13   For Koreans' names, except when they appear differently in published form this study will use the standard Korean order of surname first, followed by hyphenated given names.

14   Yong-Jo Ha, *Envisioning an Apostolic Church: Onnuri's Church Theory and Pastoral Philosophy*. Seoul: Duranno Press, 2008.

15   As Andrew Walls has put it, "We need each other's vision to correct, enlarge, and focus our own; only together we are complete in Christ"; and, "The Christianity community across the world is one." Andrew F. Walls, "The Ephesian Moment: At a Crossroads in Christian History," Ch. 4 in *The Cross-Cultural Process in Christian History: Studies in the Transmission and Appropriation of Faith*. Maryknoll, NY: Orbis Books, 2002, 80; and, "Andrew Walls: An exciting period in Christian history" *Faith & Leadership*, June 5, 2011, available online at https://www.faithandleadership.com/multimedia/andrew-walls-exciting-period-christian-history.

16   Grayson, 8-11; Lee, 19-20.

The Korean Catholic Church was certainly affected,[17] as were the mid-twentieth-century beginnings of such early and widely known Korean megachurches as Yoido Full Gospel Church[18] and Youngnak Presbyterian Church.[19] OCC founding pastor Ha Yong-jo, born in 1946, along with OCC's early church members endured those same times of suffering leading up to the church's mid-1980s founding. Pastor Ha also suffered from numerous illnesses throughout his lifetime, having multiple surgeries and hospitalizations, eventually dying at age 65 after collapsing from cerebral hemorrhaging. As one acquaintance noted to him once, "Pastor Ha, you're like a mobile hospital."[20]

It was against this backdrop of both national and Pastor Ha's personal suffering that OCC was born and developed. That suffering has shaped OCC's mission orientation in numerous ways, including inculcating compassion, humility, capacity to endure hardship, and resolute faith in God's faithfulness. In Pastor Ha's words, "As large and wonderful as Onnuri Church may seem today, it was born out of a struggle against sickness and disease. This is why I make it a point to encourage our pastors to always make time to minister to the sick and suffering."[21] It is also largely why OCC's sacrificial spirit of mission service developed the way that it has, as we will discuss further below.

Revivals

Korean Church growth (including that of OCC) has been part of worldwide church growth, almost always associated with revivals or what are

17   See, for example, article #14 entitled "Catholic Church in Korea in the 1960's" in the aforementioned Catholic Bishops' Conference of Korea series: "… both the Korean society and the [Catholic] Church at that time were challenged by serious poverty."

18   Yoido Church's humble beginnings under a tent in the rain, begun by Pastor Cho Yonggi and his future mother-in-law Pastor Choi Jashil, are well-documented. See the church's website's historical account at "About Us – History – The Tent Church," http://english.fgtv.com/a1/a1_06.asp, along with the church's informative introductory video also available online at http://english.fgtv.com/a1/a1_07.asp.

19   As noted, for example, in the church's English-language brochure (see pp. 3, 12; available online at http://homepagemedia.youngnak.net/doc/brochure_en.pdf) and in a recent article by a visiting U.S.-American researcher (Andrew Johnson, "A Crisis of Integrity in Seoul, the Megachurch Capital of the World," USC Dornsdife, Center for Religion and Civic Culture, February 9, 2016; available online at https://crcc.usc.edu/a-crisis-of-integrity-in-seoul-the-megachurch-capital-of-the-world/), Youngnak Church began in the mid-1940s by serving and gathering refugees fleeing southward from Soviet-held northern Korea.

20   Ha, 54.

21   Ibid., 55.

sometimes termed "awakenings" or "charismatic people movements."[22] The 1907 Pyongyang Revival, along with the explosive Korean Christian growth in the latter-twentieth-century aftermath of the Korean War, were examples of several recent (particularly twentieth-century) revival movements worldwide, including in North America, the Pacific Islands, Wales, England, China, Indonesia, and all parts of Sub-Saharan Africa.[23]

Having itself been born out of revival, OCC's prayers and mission initiatives particularly seek "revival" among peoples where they focus. One prominent example is OCC's "Love Sonata" musical-evangelistic outreach, or "cultural missions rally,"[24] held in cities throughout Japan over the past decade. The name was borrowed from the popular TV drama "Winter Sonata."[25] OCC's satellite TV station (CGNTV) and publishing company (Duranno Press) began, and have remained, as supporting partners.[26] Held 26 times up through 2016, the Love Sonata was begun in 2007 in connection with the centennial celebration of the 1907 Pyongyang Revival and OCC's New Year's 40-day early-morning prayer gatherings.[27] Along with reconciliation, missions, and culture, "revival" is one of four stated aspects of the Love Sonata, also described as "God's Dream" and "God's Love Song for Japan." Interestingly, "Revival Japan" is the only aspect (of the four stated aspects) included in internal (but not external) depictions of the Love Sonata logo.[28]

---

22   Michael J. McClymond, "Christian Revival and Renewal Movements," Ch. 20 in Lamin Sanneh and Michael J. McClymond, eds., *The Wiley Blackwell Companion to World Christianity*. Hoboken: Wiley, 2016, 244.

23   Many published accounts focus only on Wales, North America, and sometimes Korea. In a refreshing manner, most I have listed here (plus some others) are briefly described on the "Measure of Gold Revival Ministries" website by Evan Wiggs, http://www.evanwiggs.com/history.html. Further information about many of these revivals and others is readily available, e.g., the East African revival as described by Kevin Ward at http://www.dacb.org/stories/uganda/histories/uganda-balokole.html. Along with other AIC (African Independent Church) developments, I would include the far-reaching evangelistic ministry of William Wade Harris as a significant West African contribution, described for example by David A. Shank at http://www.dacb.org/stories/liberia/legacy_harris.html. Perhaps the most authoritative recent English-language summary of revivals worldwide is McClymond, 244-262.

24   Ha, 356. See also the OCC website (English version) at http://en.onnuri.org/missions/acts-29-ministry/.

25   Cf., for example, http://english.visitkorea.or.kr/enu/CU/CU_EN_8_5_1_1.jsp.

26   Ha, 349, 353, 372. Note as well the CGNTV and Duranno logos on the bottom of each page of the Love Sonata website, http://www.lovesonata.org/.

27   Ha, 341-342, 349-350.

28   Compare the logo on the church websites http://en.onnuri.org/missions/acts-29-ministry/ and http://www.onnuri.org/missions/acts29-ministry/love-sonata/ with that on

In noting that "revival" aspect of the Love Sonata, Pastor Ha made a direct connection with the 1907 Pyongyang Revival.[29] Furthermore, Pastor Ha's testimony was that "When I first envisioned the Love Sonata, I could only see Japan. I only thought of the revival of the Japanese church. But as Love Sonata progressed, the Lord showed me his huge vision little by little" such that "God's vision for His Kingdom became clear." Including China, India, Muslim nations, and "unreached tribes that are subject to the Muslim world," the complete "Mosaic Vision" that came to Pastor Ha was that "From Okinawa to Hokkaido, we want the sound of God's heartfelt Love Sonata to ring across the earth."[30]

Hence one basic feature of OCC's mission orientation is the posture that, just as God had used Western missionaries to bless Korea with revival, so would he use OCC's fervent prayers, various programs, and untiring initiatives – perhaps especially including the Love Sonata – to bless the whole world with a similar but even grander revival.

Economy

In a 2015 interview, the Ukrainian Ambassador to South Korea, Vasyl Marmazov, offered an insightful analysis into Korea's 1970s-1980s economic transformation, dubbed the "Miracle on the Han River." Marmarov pointed first and foremost to "the mentality of the Korean people and its values based on the Confucian ethics and moral [sic].... [In other words,] the peculiarities, the individual features of the Korean people who are distinguished because of their ability to work and high organization. The most important thing is that they saw a concrete goal and they have achieved it." He also noted the South Korean leadership's "political will," particularly that of President Park Chung-hee (1963-1979),[31] that had to take "certain harsh administrative measures" but "produced a needed result on the whole." Finally there was South Korea's realization "that they would not cope with the renewal of the country and integration in the world

http://www.lovesonata.org/.

29   Ha, 372-373. These four aspects are also stated on the Love Sonata website (in both Korean and Japanese) at http://www.lovesonata.org/introduction/lovesonata/ and http://www.lovesonata.org/ja/紹介/ラブ・ソナタ

30   Ha, 371-373.

31   For one detailed political and economic analysis, see the 2003 Institute for International Economics report, "The Miracle with a Dark Side: Korean Economic Development under Park Chung-hee," available online at https://piie.com/publications/chapters_preview/341/2iie3373.pdf.

economic system on their own. Therefore they actively involved the international aid from certain countries and international financial structures that supported South Korea." Primarily Korean qualities and determination, supported by political will and the reception of international aid, enabled South Korea to become the economic powerhouse it has become.[32]

OCC began and grew along with the burgeoning South Korean economy. Pastor Ha's calling to return to Korea from England in 1984 and start a new church (OCC) was sparked by an offered gift made one year earlier of a prime plot of real estate off the northern bank of the Han River near the heart of Seoul, in Seobinggo. That offer came from a Christian layman who was with the Shindongah Construction Company,[33] today a significant and vibrant corporation founded in 1977.[34] Such wealth associated with the dramatic growth of the Korean economy has helped to fund not only OCC's significant building projects but also the many different mission initiatives that OCC has undertaken. This same phenomenon has occurred in many other Korean churches' growth and the corresponding rise of the overall Korean missions movement.

It was 150 years ago that U.S.-American mission leader Rufus Anderson noted Providential orchestration of global political and economic events to open unevangelized countries to Western Christian missionaries.[35] Today, a similar correlation between the rise in the Korean economy and South Korea's international stature on the one hand, and Korean church growth and the explosive increase of Korean missionaries on the other hand, has not been lost on both outside analysts and Korean Christians alike. While such a relationship no doubt has also involved other factors already mentioned, that correlation has been regularly noted by

---

32   Mykola Siruk, "On the three factors of 'The Miracle on the Han River,'" April 23, 2015, available online at https://day.kyiv.ua/en/article/economy/three-factors-miracle-han-river.

33   Ha, 8; *Onnuri Community Church: The First 30 Years*. Publisher, Jae-hoon Lee. English Translation Editor-in-Chief, J. Nelson Jennings. Onnuri Community Church, 2015 (English Translation, 2017), 115-116. (At the time of writing, a revised English version was being planned.)

34   See the Shindongah Engineering & Construction English-language online brochure at http://www.sdaconst.co.kr/eng/Company/History.asp.

35   Rufus Anderson, *Foreign Missions: Their Relations and Claims*. New York: Charles Scribner and Company, 1869. Note especially Ch. 1, "An Opening World," 1-15. Available online at https://openlibrary.org/books/OL23413170M/Foreign_missions_their_relations_and_claims.

Korean Christians to be God's blessing on Korea,[36] including in order for Koreans to carry forward the torch of Christian missions. As OCC founding pastor Ha Yong-jo preached at OCC's eleventh anniversary celebration (and adoption of eight unreached people groups), "Just as the salvation of Christ transformed this land, I believe that in 50, 60, 100 years, the nations you all bless will also reflect the blessings Korea has received,"[37] including Korea's recent economic growth.

Diaspora

The current Korean diaspora is not as large as those as those of India, Mexico, Russia, China, Bangladesh, or 20 other countries.[38] Remarkably, however, according to the Overseas Korean Foundation people of Korean descent are settled in 175 countries, making them the most widespread diaspora in the world.[39] As such, the Korean diaspora is thus part of a worldwide phenomenon. For its part, modern Korean emigration began in the 1860s northward into Russia as well as China, then accelerated in the early 1900s to the Americas and then to Japan-ruled territories under the 1910-1945 Japanese Occupation. Emigration patterns became more varied after Korean independence, including a large thrust to the United States after its 1965 Immigration Reform Act of 1965 and another increase to China after the 1992 normalization of diplomatic relations between China and South Korea.[40]

Throughout world history, religious groups have spread with the emigration of diasporas, including the earliest Christians scattered by persecution.[41] The spread

---

36   "Christianity in Korea," in *New World Encyclopedia*, available online at http://www.newworldencyclopedia.org/entry/Christianity_in_Korea. Anecdotally, I have heard this testimony numerous times, both explicitly and implicitly.

37   Ha, 286-287.

38   According to UN mid-2015 statistics available online at http://www.un.org/en/development/desa/population/migration/data/estimates2/data/UN_MigrantStockByOriginAndDestination_2015.xlsx (Table 16). The Korean diaspora is listed as 2,345,840, with India's as the highest at 15,575,724.

39   In accordance with Ministry of Foreign Affairs 2011 statistics claiming 7.26 million Koreans worldwide. "World's widest diaspora born over 100 years ago" *Korea Joongang Daily* October 2, 2013, available online at http://koreajoongangdaily.joins.com/news/article/Article.aspx?aid=2978298. Clearly how the data is counted varies between the UN figures just cited and these Ministry of Foreign Affairs figures. Presumably the difference lies in where migrants were born. In any case, the relative rankings offered can be assumed to be correct on their own terms.

40   "Korean diaspora" *New World Encyclopedia*, Available online at http://www.newworldencyclopedia.org/entry/Korean_diaspora.

41   Acts 8:1, 4; 11:19-21.

of Islam into Southeast Asia, particularly from the thirteenth century onward, is another easily identifiable example, in this instance of traders soon accompanied by Sufi mystics.[42] The Christian Modern Missions Movement, stretching from the late-fifteenth to the mid-twentieth centuries, can also be understood in connection with the emigration of a European diaspora throughout the world together with Catholic, Orthodox, and various Protestant emissaries.[43] The triangular post-World War II breakup of European Empires, twentieth-century explosion of non-Western Christian growth (including in Sub-Saharan Africa and Korea), and accelerated, multidirectional growth of diasporas worldwide has seen, among other religious developments, the growth of international Christian networks in connection with corresponding diaspora networks, be they Chinese, Nigerian, Brazilian, Ghanaian, Korean, or otherwise.

OCC's international growth through the establishment of its association of "Vision Churches" is one of many such Korean international networks that have developed in tandem with the Korean diaspora. Accordingly, 25 of OCC's currently 30 Vision Churches are in Japan, China, and North America, with the other five also among Koreans living in Abu Dhabi, Vietnam, New Zealand, Guam, and Sydney.[44] These Vision Churches are a fundamental part of OCC's overall mission orientation, taking shape within Korean peoples emigrating according to historically typical factors of economics, political initiatives, and war.

Non-Korean diasporas have included increased numbers entering South Korea as well. The 1992 normalization of relations between China and South Korea fostered an acceleration in the immigration of Chinese, including Chinese of Korean descent, into South Korea. Many other nationalities have also been entering South Korea as its economic growth has provided (and demanded) new opportunities for work, education, or arranged marriages to Koreans. Accordingly, since 1993 OCC has responded with ever-expanding ministries to new international arrivals through

---

42   "Islam From The Beginning To 1300: The Spread Of Islam To Southeast Asia" *International World History Project: World History From The Pre-Sumerian Period To The Present. A Collection Of World History Related Essays, Documents, Maps and Music*, available online at http://history-world.org/islam7.htm; Imtiyaz Yusuf, "The Middle East and Muslim Southeast Asia: Implications of the Arab Spring" *Oxford Islamic Studies Online*, available online at http://www.oxfordislamicstudies.com/Public/focus/essay1009_southeast_asia.html.

43   I acknowledge Andrew Walls as the first scholar I heard asserting this framework of understanding.

44   *Onnuri Community Church: The First 30 Years*, 132-135.

its "M Mission" ("Migrant Mission"), a focus that is drawing increased attention within OCC's mission orientation.[45]

The lives of both OCC Senior Pastors are interconnected with major phases of the Korean diaspora. Born in 1946 in northern Korea, Ha Yong-jo fled southward with his Christian parents and siblings in 1951 during the Korean War. He traveled with his wife to England for three years in the early 1980s for study and rest. His periodic travels to Hawaii and to Japan for health reasons fit other Koreans' travel patterns.[46] As for Pastor Lee Jae-hoon, like many other Koreans of his generation he has spent significant periods in the U.S., in his case both as a student at Trinity Evangelical Divinity School in Illinois and as a pastor in New Jersey. Both men's displacements and mobile sojourns have been microcosms of the overall Korean diaspora, including in the deep affect given to OCC's mission orientation.

OCC Features

Listing particular features of OCC that distinguish its mission orientation is fraught with challenges. One challenge is that such labels and categories inevitably overlap with each other, as well as intersect with other sections of this study. Another is that a limited list of features unavoidably omit several other items that could be included.[47] Here I have settled on four features that can both incorporate other distinguishing features as well as present OCC's mission approaches in a manner that I believe is accurate, understandable, and manageable.

The Holy Spirit

Listing the Holy Spirit here is in no sense intended to imply that other churches, including other megachurches, have not experienced or emphasized the Spirit the way that OCC has. Even just a cursory glance at other churches in Korea and worldwide quickly dispels any notion of OCC having had any sort of monopoly on the Spirit's blessing, presence, and work. Rather, the prominence of

---

45   In collaboration with OCC colleagues, I have written about OCC's M Mission in a forthcoming publication's chapter, "Reverse Migration Ministries from Korea: A Case Study of Onnuri Community Church's M Mission."

46   Ha, 27-94.

47   For this list, other features I considered using included the Bible, OCC's own mission agency TIM (Tyrannus International Mission), both the "Acts 29" and "2000/10000" vision statements, and others. Within this limited study I decided that these categories could effectively be examined in connection with others.

the Spirit's role in OCC's mission orientation demands explicit attention here in describing OCC's particular features.

First, I affirm the Holy Spirit's presence and work among and through OCC and its mission initiatives. The fruit of the Spirit is evident, the gifts of the Spirit (e.g., in Ephesians 4) are undeniable, the presence of the Spirit among OCC individuals and gatherings is real, and the ministry fruit in peoples' lives that have been changed – many of whom I have met personally – are abundantly confirmed by testimony and renewed lifestyles. The work of God's Spirit throughout the earth and across the generations has included forming and enlisting OCC in His mission.

Second, OCC leaders and members consciously depend on the Holy Spirit for guidance and empowerment; and, they testify that the Spirit leads and empowers OCC's mission, vision, programs, and efforts. I have been privy to many aspects of this dependence and testimony, for example in leaders' consistent refrain that OCC's foundation consists of "The Word and Spirit," as well as in the plethora of regular prayer groups devoted to OCC mission causes. Moreover, published records of OCC history and Pastor Ha's own accounts point to the Spirit as having shaped and empowered OCC and its mission.

Having been led by God's Spirit to learn several invaluable lessons before and during their three years in England,[48] during their last year there Pastor Ha and his wife prayed about starting a new church on the offered plot of land in Seobinggo. Their testimony is that God showed Ha a vision of the Early Church in Acts and the need, amidst the myriad churches already in Korea, for "the very Church" of Acts to be planted in Seoul.[49] One can see at work here a "This is that!" hermeneutic by which Pentecostals have "collapsed the presumed distinction between the scriptural text and its contemporary readers," opting for the Bible's "capacity to open up possibilities for contemporary readers and hearers by the power of the Spirit."[50] Seven years after returning to Seoul in 1984 and seeing that church begin to develop, due to illness Pastor Ha went to Hawaii for a sabbatical. Pastor Ha testified later, "As soon as I got off the plane [in Hawaii], I felt God's voice strongly

---

48   Ha, 73-90.

49   *Onnuri Community Church: The First 30 Years*, 116-117.

50   Amos Yong, "Reading Scripture and Nature: Pentecostal Hermeneutics and Their Implications for the Contemporary Evangelical Theology and Science Conversation" *Perspectives on Science and Christian Faith* 63(1), March, 2011, 4-5, available online at http://www.asa3.org/ASA/PSCF/2011/PSCF3-11Yong.pdf.

saying just one thing, 'Start a Pentecostal movement. Use the Holy Spirit in your ministry.'" After praying in Hawaii, "I will not go back until I receive Your anointing, Your Holy Fire. Allow me to experience that same Holy Spirit that descended upon Your disciples on the Pentecost," Pastor Ha assembled the OCC leadership upon his 1992 return to Seoul and "shared with them my vision for a charismatic ministry: a ministry driven by the Holy Spirit." A two-day revival conference entitled "Come, Holy Spirit!" was held, and OCC's explosive growth ensued.[51]

Per Pastor Ha's testimony, "As we began to accept the work of the Holy Spirit, as a foggy camera clears, our vision also became clear before our eyes." In particular, "The Lord has given Onnuri a great vision to commission 2,000 missionaries and train 10,000 lay leaders by the year 2010. That vision was made clear in 1994."[52] OCC's permeating "Acts 29" vision, to continue to write the Book of Acts by being "the very Church" conveyed there, was declared by Pastor Ha in 2003,[53] flowing out of the Spirit's showing him connections between Acts and his experiences of illness. Then "At the end of 2007, I received a vision from God to go to Japan with all of Onnuri's resources to win it over for Christ," Ha wrote about the origin of the Love Sonata.[54]

While the Word and Spirit may together comprise OCC's foundation, Pastor Ha and OCC particularly acknowledge the Spirit's work of envisioning, empowering, and otherwise blessing them for mission.[55]

Leadership

Pastor Ha's testimony about the Spirit includes instructions about leadership: "The most important factor in biblical leadership is the anointing of the Holy Spirit." And, "The salvation of this earth is in the hands of God's leaders."[56] A central factor in determining OCC's particular mission orientation has been leadership, namely the particular leaders involved.

---

51   Ha, 90-93.

52   Ha, 280.

53   *Onnuri Community Church: The First 30 Years*, 49-50, 128; "Onnuri Church History," available on the OCC website (English version) at http://en.onnuri.org/about-onnuri/onnuri-church-history/.

54   Ha, 341.

55   OCC's "charismatic" character, including such "sign" gifts as healings and glosso-lalia, is discussed under the "megachurch" section below.

56   Ha, 317.

Founding and long-time Senior Pastor Ha Yong-jo has been the central leader in shaping OCC's mission character. Much of this study focuses on him and his experience, since in its ongoing mission program OCC continues to focus on Pastor Ha's example and teaching as well. A prime example is how the curricula for OCC's three main missionary training programs all begin with a study of Pastor Ha's philosophy of mission.[57] In general, Pastor Ha remains much beloved and deeply revered among OCC members and mission leaders.[58]

Other individuals have also been vitally important as developers of OCC mission emphases. One was Missionary Samuel Kim. Having been approved as the first Korean Christian and Missionary Alliance missionary, Kim started seven churches in Japan (1983-1992), fostered the translation of BEE (Bible Education by Extension) materials for Chinese church leaders (1993-1997), then served in Korea as OCC's head of missionary training (1998-2004), including as director of the Onnuri Mission Training Center (now Acts 29 Vision Village). Kim died of cancer soon after leading a team of missionaries to Iraq.[59] Another influential mission leader has been Missionary Stephen Ha, Pastor Ha's brother. Having been influenced in worship by the same Baptist church in England as Pastor Ha, not long after OCC had begun Stephen Ha returned to Seoul and led praise and worship at OCC, including a large and influential Thursday evening service for young adults. All Nations Worship and Praise Ministries (ANWPM) soon emerged, infusing OCC's life and mission with a "dynamic mix of praise, prayer and preaching."[60] All Nations Worship and Praise Institutes (with several campuses located internationally) also developed, along with traveling choirs and multiple worship CD's.[61]

---

57   The three programs, conducted at OCC's Acts 29 Vision Village in Yangji one hour south of Seoul, are TP ("Turning Point") for short-term missionaries, OSOM ("Onnuri School of Mission") for long-term missionaries, and H2H ("Home2Home") for missionaries on furlough.

58   For two online tributes that exemplify the outpouring of grief and appreciation after Ha Yong-jo's August 2011 death, see Eugene Cho's "in memory of pastor ha yong jo" and Eddie Byun's "Pastor Ha, Yong Jo (1946-2011)," available respectively at https://eugenecho. com/2011/08/02/in-memory-of-pastor-hah-yong-jo/ and at http://www.eddiebyun.com/ blog/pastor-ha-yong-jo-1946-2011.

59   Samuel Kim's biography was written by his widow Young S. Kim, *The King's Invitation*. Seoul: Duranno Press, 2011. His life and career is succinctly summarized in the first 12 slides of a PowerPoint presentation compiled in 2004 by Jintae Kim, entitled "Samuel Kim and Getting it done in Korea or by Koreans," available on the www.all4jesus.net website.

60   Ha, 169.

61   *Onnuri Community Church: The First 30 Years*, 344-347. For a flavor of the fervency and style of the praise and worship that developed starting in the mid-1980s, see

In concert with Pastor Ha's emphasis on lay leadership have been the major roles played by numerous lay leaders in executing OCC's mission. Reference was made earlier to Elder Choi Soon-young of Shindongah Corporation, who donated land in Seobinggo for OCC's first and main campus. In addition, Choi's similar leadership granted facilities to other churches and organizations, including for Far Eastern Broadcasting Company-Korea[62] and Kwanglim Methodist Church.[63] Other wealthy Korean individuals have contributed significantly to major mission-related building and ministry projects. Organizationally, all throughout OCC's mission development there have been lay leaders – some of them with significant corporate and political positions – who have played prominent roles in partnership with pastors. This effective partnership is what Pastor Ha taught and embodied,[64] and it is what I have consistently observed. Stories abound of church members going to Pastor Ha with ideas for ministry projects, and his response was for them to go and start them up. The result is prominent lay leadership in all church programs, including OCC's many different mission initiatives.

Currently, the single most strategically placed OCC mission leader is Sr. Pastor Lee Jae-hoon. In many ways, Pastor Lee's intertwined spirituality, thinking, leadership, and decisions embody the crux of this study about OCC's mission orientation and related missiological discussion points. Having served under Pastor Ha for many years and in various OCC roles, Pastor Lee understands, honors, and is carrying forward OCC's mission orientation that has been shaped under Pastor Ha's influence. At the same time, Pastor Lee and OCC are in new and changing times, hence he must update and adjust certain emphases, for example by amplifying OCC's permeating "Acts 29" vision with a new phrase, "Fools for Christ."[65] What Pastor Lee faces missiologically, and how he and OCC are dealing with such realities, will continue to unfold in this study.

---

the two videos posted on February 9, 2017 at https://www.facebook.com/vision2085?hc_ref=PAGES_TIMELINE.

62   Billy Kim, *The Life of Billy Kim: From Houseboy to World Evangelist*. Chicago, IL: Moody Publishers, 2015, 130.

63   Kim Sundo, A Miracle of Five Minutes: The Autobiography of Kim Sundo. Ch. 16, "Arriving at the Summit of the Vision." Nashville, TN: Abingdon Press, 2015.

64   Ha, 110-120.

65   Details about the remarkably smooth transition from Pastor Ha to Pastor Lee are in *Onnuri Community Church: The First 30 Years*, 11-58.

Megachurch

Many testimonies of megachurch leaders insist that their churches' growth occurred suddenly and surprisingly. For example, in the early stages of Yoido Full Gospel Church people are said to have appeared "much like the gathering of rain clouds,"[66] and OCC founding pastor Ha attested that "people who began to flock to our church could only be compared to 'a cloud of locusts'."[67] Whatever the expectations or plans might have been, megachurches have mushroomed across the globe since the early twentieth century. According to the most current and definitive list of global megachurches,[68] out of today's almost 300 megachurches listed with a starting date,[69] 93% began in the last 100 years.[70] Interestingly, 52% or over half of the world's current documented megachurches began during the quarter-century between 50 and 25 years ago (1967-1992), including the Korean megachurches listed.[71]

For its part, OCC began in 1984 when Pastor Ha returned to Seoul from England and started meeting with 12 families. As such, one study puts OCC in "The Third Generation" of Korean megachurches.[72] The church grew to about 2,500 over the next six years, then exploded after Ha returned in 1992 from a sabbatical away in Hawaii because of illness. Benchmark membership numbers

---

66   Yoido Full Gospel Church website, "About Us – History – The Church at SeoDaeMun," available at http://english.fgtv.com/a1/a1_062.asp.

67   Ha, 92. The reference is to 1992, after Pastor Ha returned to Seoul having had a revolutionary experience with the Holy Spirit during a sickness-induced sabbatical in Hawaii. Writing a decade-and-a-half later he wrote, "When our church first started, I didn't expect it to grow this big. I had never dreamt of a mega-church and I had never even been part of a mega-church. I couldn't even conceive of it but here we are." Ha, 289.

68   "Global Megachurches by Leadership Network's Warren Bird, PhD (leadnet.org/world)," available online at https://docs.google.com/spreadsheets/d/1YIKShcapvO6LatV5WG7P4XXczuoaw9EAfKv3IMJwXnQ/edit?hl=en_US&hl=en_US#gid=0. Note that this list does not include North American churches, which are listed elsewhere online at http://www.hartfordinstitute.org/megachurch/database.html.

69   About 100 megachurches are listed without a founding year included.

70   For further reference and comparison, 76% began in the last 50 years and 24% during the most recent 25 years.

71   Here, "Korean" means "in Korea." There are 38 total Korean megachurches listed, 22 with founding dates. Of those 22, 55% (12) began between 1967-1992, with all other ten earlier.

72   Michael Bégin and Caleg Kwang-Eun Shin, "Sacred Ambitions, Global Dreams: Inside the Korean Megachurch Phenomenon," Ch. 122 in Stanley D. Brunn, ed., *The Changing World Religion Map: Sacred Places, Identities, Practices and Politics*. 2015 Ed. New York: Springer, 2015, 2322-2323.

reached include 6,000 (1993), 11,000 (1996), 21,000 (2000), 45,000 (2005), and 75,000 (2010), [73] graphically depicted below.

Onnuri Community Church
Membership Totals, 1984-2010

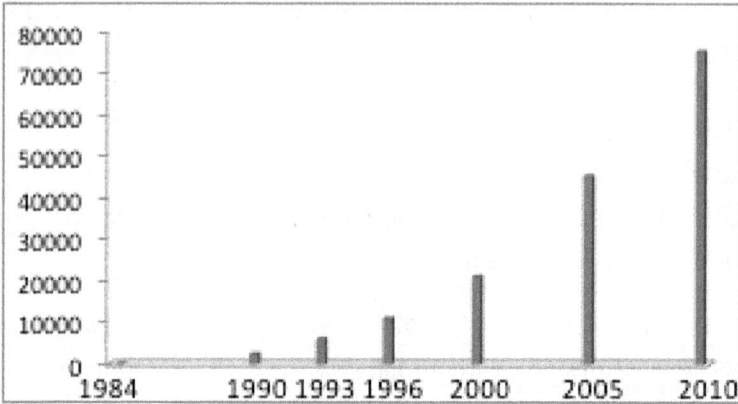

One of OCC's basic mission orientations *as a megachurch* inculcated by Pastor Ha was his emphasis on sacrificial service to others. The twin, underlying imperatives he gave were (1) share with others the blessings God had uniquely poured out on OCC, and (2) be scattered just like the earliest megachurch, the Jerusalem Church in the book of Acts, was scattered. Ha's own comments here are worth extensive quotation:

> People have come to Onnuri Church in masses. A great revival is occurring. We are blessed to be a part of this revival of Korean Christianity.... I believe that the revival God is allowing here at our church [is] the exact same sort with which God blessed the Early Church in the Book of Acts.... [After God gave growth, and as the Jews oppressed the Jerusalem church and their leaders,] The 20,000 members of the Jerusalem church [were] scattered all across the world.

---

73   According to the OCC website (English version) at http://en.onnuri.org/about-onnuri/onnuri-church-history/. The 45,000 figure and approximate 2005 date come from the aforementioned "South Korean Missionaries" 2007 documentary. The membership totals include the various OCC campuses in Korea and Vision Churches throughout the world.

As I meditated on the sufferings of the early church, God showed me what was happening, how He was working, through my life. [During my illnesses, surgeries, and accompanying meditations on Acts,] it hit me that if [we] don't scatter, we're going to be oppressed! I shared this vision with the leadership: Dear beloved leaders of Onnuri, we must not hoard and settle in this blessing and revival from God....

God has blessed us in many ways. He has given us great ministries in evangelism, discipleship, mission, worship, praise, small groups, quiet times, etc. What other church do you know of has been the recipient of such an outpour[ing] of His grace?

There are many large churches but without the right software, so to speak. Some have the right software but their hardware is inadequate. But God has blessed us with both the software and the hardware to go and scatter.

We must share these blessings.... We must find ways to spread this blessing to all the churches in Korea.[74]

Based on connecting (a) his own illnesses to the Early Church's suffering and scattering; and, (b) OCC's perceived unique (at least among Korean megachurches) combination of growth, lack of scandals or problems, and abundance of people, facilities, and programs to the same characteristics of the earliest megachurch in Jerusalem, Pastor Ha urged OCC leaders and members sacrificially to disperse and serve. In a very real sense, then, OCC's mission orientation is inherently tied to OCC as the particular megachurch that it has become.

Alongside this reality that OCC's mission orientation is inherently tied to its megachurch status are at least three other characteristics that are connected to OCC being a megachurch. First, there are myriad mission programs. In one sense, OCC considers most all of its programs as mission programs, starting with OCC's two most fundamental programs of QT ("Quiet Time" training and materials) and One-to-One discipleship.[75] These and other programs – e.g., "Father School,"

---

74   Ha, 291-293.

75   From the beginning of my acquaintance with OCC in 2012, every explanation of OCC I have been given has emphasized the fundamental place of QT and One-to-One for all members. See also *Onnuri Community Church: The First 30 Years*, 124-126, 137-142.

worship styles, Duranno Press materials – are used in OCC's various campus churches (in Korea) and Vision Churches (outside Korea), by OCC missionaries, and in direct connection with international churches and organizations. OCC's specifically mission programs are legion with several of them quite large, for example TIM (Tyrannus International Mission, OCC's own mission-sending agency or "sodality" currently with over 400 active missionaries), Acts 29 Vision Village, M ("Migrant") Mission, BEE-Korea, Better World (OCC's NGO), and CGNTV.[76] Even Duranno Press, one of Korea's major Christian publishing companies, was conceived by Pastor Ha as part of OCC's mission by "supplying healthy Christian contents" to people worldwide.[77]

Second, since 2015 OCC's mission leaders (most especially elders) have discussed and implemented a "convergence" approach to OCC mission. In one sense, OCC's "convergence" mission is a wider, international extension of Pastor Ha's "matrix" model of collaboration and free movement between OCC campuses, Vision churches, and related organizations.[78] In the wake of a 2013 reorganization of the elder committee structure (now with 15 subcommittees, one of which is "overseas missions" although many others overlap with mission concerns),[79] and in light of a plateauing Korean economy that motivates more careful monitoring of budgets,[80] OCC's mission leaders have sought greater overall effectiveness through planning and collaboration between mission programs, in consultation with missionaries in touch with field needs. Along with being a management strategy, OCC's "convergence" mission fits a historical and sociological pattern for

---

76   Of these major examples, only TIM, Acts 29 VV, and the M Mission are "fully" OCC entities, since the others have their own independent organizational status and boards. Effectively, however, especially with Sr. Pastor Lee Jae-hoon as their official corporate head, all these entities are substantially OCC programs financially and personnel-wise. There are several other noteworthy specifically mission programs, including the Ezer Prayer Ministry and SWIM (Society for World Internet Mission). The aforementioned All Nations Worship and Praise Ministries has developed into more of an independent and internationally-based missions organization (cf. Ha, 311).

77   See "Introduction" on the Duranno Press website (English version) at http://www.duranno.com/english/introduce.asp. Note that "Duranno" and "Tyrannus" of TIM are the same word from Acts 19.

78   Ha, 307-311.

79   *Onnuri Community Church: The First 30 Years*, 42.

80   Even with a Korea's economic slowdown, pledges to OCC overseas missions– annually collected in early January – have increased.

any organization, be it a nation-state or a small group of friends, to consolidate its identity and programs following an intense period of accelerated growth.[81]

A third trait of OCC's megachurch status is its "Big Tent" capacity to incorporate a wide range of themes and organizations, some of which can seem contradictory. Denominationally speaking, OCC is part of the Presbyterian Church of Korea (PCK, or *Tonghap*),[82] which in turn is affiliated with the Korean National Council of Churches (KNCC).[83] The PCK is one of the largest among the bewildering array of Korean Presbyterian denominations.[84] Organizationally and missiologically, however, OCC connects more with the Lausanne Movement. OCC functions in this kind of all-embracing way against the backdrop of its all-encompassing "Acts 29" vision. For example, in explaining how OCC functions as a "multi-site church" with several campuses in Korea and even more Vision Churches internationally, Pastor Ha noted that "None of our churches are bound by denominations but rather by the vision of Acts 29. All our churches aim to continue writing the 29th chapter of the Book of Acts until Jesus returns."[85] Furthermore, OCC's various pastors themselves are ordained in a wide variety of denominations. It is the OCC-as-megachurch's Acts 29 vision (and updated "Fools for Christ" vision) that provides the unifying, umbrella vision for OCC's various denominational connections as OCC and as OCC pastors.

OCC's approximately 900 missionaries are hence connected with a variety of mission agencies. About half are with OCC's own TIM, and about half are spread out among a wide array of other agencies (including some with Better World and other OCC-related entities). Similarly, OCC has embraced "Charismatic" expressions of worship as well as such "sign" gifts as glossolalia

---

81   Examples abound, including Japan's mid-Meiji consolidation (1889 Meiji Constitution and 1990 Imperial Rescript on Education) following its two decades of dizzying absorption of all things Western and accelerated growth into a modern economic and military empire.

82   The PCK *Tonghap* English website is at http://www.pck.or.kr/Eng/Main/engMain. asp. During one of my numerous interviews with OCC staff and members, the origin of OCC's *Tonghap* affiliation was explained to lie in Pastor Ha's relationships with *Tonghap* leaders who, like him, had northern Korean roots.

83   The KNCC, like other national church councils, is WCC-affiliated.

84   One helpful succinct explanation of the many Korean Presbyterian churches, including some background for the plethora of splits and groups, is on the "Korea, Republic of" web page of the *Reformed Online* website at http://www.reformiert-online. net/weltweit/75_eng.php.

85   Ha, 310.

and healings, without being classified within or belonging to any particular "Charismatic" or "Pentecostal" organization. Furthermore, OCC as a megachurch can simultaneously relate to seemingly contradictory groups, including Chinese house churches and government-recognized churches as well as more theologically "Reformed" teaching and a dispensational, current-state-of-Israel-supporting Korea Israel Bible Institute (KIBI).

In sum, OCC's mission orientation is a collaborative, multi-program array of initiatives inherently connected to OCC the Acts 29 megachurch.

The Name "Onnuri"

Having considered OCC's distinguishing mission features of the Spirit, its leadership, and megachurch traits, it is also instructive to note a fourth particular trait in relation to OCC's mission orientation, namely the designation "*Onnuri.*" That name is written in *Hangul* (the Korean script) as 온누리. In Chinese characters, it is written as 大地.[86] In other languages the term is simply transliterated. The consistent English meaning that the church conveys is "All Nations," referring to the Matthew 28:19 centerpiece of Jesus' Great Commission to "Make disciples of all nations."[87] OCC's mission orientation is thus expressed in its very name, *Onnuri.*

The term is a purely Korean word, meaning that it was not borrowed from any other language – including Chinese, from which a large portion of Korean terms originate. The word is a combination of 온 (*on*, "all") and 누리 (*nuri*, "world"), the latter particularly being the purely Korean term. Additionally, the word is an older term that is no longer in common use. Another important matter is that the term itself does not actually appear anywhere in any Korean version of Bible, including in Matthew 28:19. Other Korean phrases (with Chinese origins) that linguistically express more faithfully and accurately the Greek phrase in Matthew 28:19, πάντα τὰ ἔθνη (*panta ta ethne*, or "all the nations/peoples"), are used there.[88]

---

86   See the Chinese version of the OCC website at http://cn.onnuri.org/. The only other occasion I have ever seen the term written in Chinese characters has been on a road sign in Yangjae, pointing to the church's campus location at Torch Trinity Graduate University.

87   Ha, 111, 281-282; *Onnuri Community Church: The First 30 Years*, 238.

88   For example, 모든 족속 (*modeun joksok*).

Linguistically speaking, a closer English equivalent to 온누리 (onnuri) than "all nations" would be "the whole world," or perhaps "the entire creation."[89] Taking a lead from the Chinese-equivalent 大地, "grand land" would be another option. As for specific Scriptures where 온누리 would thus be a closer linguistic match than in Matthew 28:19, כָּל־הָאָרֶץ ("all the earth") in Psalm 66:1, 4, πάσῃ τῇ κτίσει ("the whole creation") in Mark 16:15, and πᾶσαν τὴν οἰκουμένην ("all the world") in, e.g., Luke 2:1 come to mind. Here again, though, other phrases (with Chinese origins) are used in Korean Bibles rather than 온누리.[90] For whatever reasons, Korean Bible translators have not chosen the term *onnuri* to convey any biblical phrases, including in Matthew 28:19.[91]

Why then did Pastor Ha use, and in turn why has OCC continued to use, 온누리 (*onnuri*) with a mission orientation consciously connected to the "all nations" of Matthew 28:19 in the Great Commission? That question may be impossible to answer fully, but I believe that traveling down two avenues of understanding this situation prove constructive. One is to realize that a "linguistically faithful and accurate" translation may not convey the intended meaning in a certain context as much as a "faithful, appropriate, and relevant" translation would.[92] For this discussion, the clear fact that 온누리 (*onnuri*) is not as linguistically faithful and accurate as other Korean phrases (especially including in contemporary usage) does not therefore rule out being able to use the term in some connection with Matthew 28:19.

The second avenue of understanding explains even more why Pastor Ha and OCC have used that phrase with a Great Commission-related intention. The first three traits examined here that have shaped OCC's particular mission orientation – the Spirit, the leaders, and OCC-as-megachurch – gave rise to *Onnuri* Community Church developing its particular mission orientation. Living and leading as the Founding Senior Pastor of OCC, Ha Yong-jo exemplified his own understanding and description of "Being filled with the Holy Spirit" and the development of OCC:

---

89   See, for example, translations given using the online dictionaries at http://www.lexicool.com/korean-dictionary-translation.asp.

90   For example, 온 땅이여 (*on ttang-i-yeo*) and 온 세상이 (*on se-sang-i*) in Psalm 66, and 모든 사람 (*modeun saram*) in Mark 16.

91   I have listed these various translations and Scriptural examples after my own research and after conferring with two Korean colleagues (one a pastor in the OCC matrix and the other a missionary who knows OCC quite well) and Andrew Walls.

92   I am borrowing here from the insightful study by Daniel R. Shaw and Charles E. Van Engen, *Communicating God's Word in a Complex World: God's Truth or Hocus Pocus?* Oxford: Rowman & Littlefield Publishers, 2003.

> You receive fire, you receive power, you experience the anointing of the Holy Spirit and you allow the Holy Spirit to act through you. You speak the words that the Spirit gives you. Speech is thought and without thought, language does not exist.[93] When I am filled with the Holy Spirit, I act on the will of the Holy Spirit and I represent the Holy Spirit. People who are filled with the Spirit will attract people who are hungry for the Spirit, people who want to be filled with the Spirit. This is revival![94]

Pastor Ha's ever-growing, Spirit-inspired vision was that the church based in Seoul, South Korea that he would begin and then lead would carry forward the torch lit in the first century until *onnuri*, the whole and entire world, would be a realization of the Spirit-filled, heavenly dream he had for all people. That was Ha Yong-jo's dream and vision that developed along with *Onnuri*-as-megachurch. It was his, and continues to be OCC's, deeply spiritual sense of calling to share the *Onnuri* revival that God has given them. Sacrificially serving toward realizing that vision is the only viable outcome for that calling.

OCC is Korean

OCC's historical context of suffering, revivals, the Korean economy, and people in diaspora have shaped its mission orientation. The Holy Spirit, OCC leaders, OCC's megachurch character, and OCC's *Onnuri* identity have combined to distinguish OCC's mission orientation. What, then, does OCC's Korean character mean for its mission orientation?

To state the obvious (and to note some qualifications), OCC is a *Korean* megachurch. There are obvious international and non-Korean elements – for example, worship services take place each Sunday in Russian, Chinese, Japanese, English, and in connection with OCC's growing M Mission several other Asian languages – but the operative language, structure, historical context, and heritage of the vast majority of leaders, participants, and activities is Korean. Many lay leaders and pastors have significant international life experience, but the vast majority of OCC's population is Korean in character. Various materials are translated into, and

---

93   Perhaps a smoother English translation for this sentence would shift the comma forward: "Speech is thought, and without thought language does not exist."

94   Ha, 133.

in some cases originally produced in, non-Korean languages – the church website's English/Japanese/Chinese versions, Duranno Press, and CGNTV, to name the most prominent examples – but the bulk and foundation of materials are in Korean. Again, while bearing the worldwide marks of its character as *Onnuri* Community Church, OCC is a *Korean* megachurch.

Besides being obvious, OCC's Korean character is normal. Particular churches have contextual homes, including megachurches. That is how God has shaped and developed churches throughout history.

Aspects

For OCC, then, one major emphasis – by committee structure, ongoing prayers, special prayer events, and targeted ministries – is Korea reunification.[95] Another is the fervent and frequent prayer gatherings, including well-known large pre-dawn meetings. Exuberance and open expression in worship (culturally relative as such qualities might be), including intensity in preaching, are also displayed.

While not unique to Korea, other Korean features include church-wide use of the same daily QT materials, similar attire worn on Sunday by select groups (pastors and elders, choir members, ushers, offering presenters, etc.), ongoing honoring of the founding pastor (e.g., on the church website, airing of recorded sermons, annual memorial services), and hierarchical communication and decision-making structures (albeit modified by the leveled leadership that both senior pastors have cultivated and practiced).

Implications via an Example

Some implications of these aspects of OCC's Korean character for its mission orientation can be illustrated and teased out by an example from the July 2007 Tokyo Love Sonata, beginning with Pastor Ha's own account:

> It was like a dream come true. Our church has been preparing for months and we poured out all our resources into making it a success. The atmosphere inside the Saitama Super Arena was electric. Our members began setting up for the evening event since 9:00 in the morning and they were filled with excitement. 5,000

---

95   *Onnuri Community Church: The First 30 Years*, 42.

Korean Christians had been waiting for this day since the 40 days of early morning-prayer. Many had paid their own way. All had come to Japan with a vision. A vision of reconciliation and unity.

Pastor Ha then recounted the various events and meetings involved with the entire Tokyo Love Sonata, including its trademark "special performance by our Korean Christian celebrities."[96]

Adjoining Ha's remarks are these comments by a Japanese senior pastor of a Japanese church:

> The Love Sonata had created a 'holy illusion'. I had forgotten that I was in Tokyo. It felt like I was in Seoul at Onnuri Church! It seemed as if [your] lay ministers had been with us from the very beginning helping, encouraging and supporting in any way they could. I truly felt like one community; a community of Christ, bound together by love.

> The people of Onnuri Church served Japan humbly and selflessly. Even the women and the weak bodied served us with all their hearts. Japanese people are uncomfortable when we receive in such abundance! It's part of our culture to give something in return. But we have nothing we can offer to Onnuri. The only thing we can promise is to hold fast to the love that we received and live a life pleasing to God.

Ensuing comments by other participants convey gratitude, encouragement, and fresh resolve for gospel service – including the last comment by another Japanese pastor: "I have such great hopes because of the Love Sonata! I was so touched by the message and when we threw our paper airplanes into the air! I felt God's love through the people and the entire event!"[97]

The following characteristics (descriptive, not necessarily evaluative) emerge from this Love Sonata sketch, with particular reference to the Korean character of OCC's mission orientation and practice:

---

96   Ha, 361-363.
97   Ha, 363-370.

- Fervent prayer permeates the preparation.
- Mission service is rooted in a strong sense of calling.
- Humility, sacrifice, and full-fledged passion characterize the service rendered.
- Korean leadership and initiative energize the activities.
- Korean people and resources supply the needed materials.
- Korean cultural traits of color, music, and expression mark the event.
- Gospel fruit is evident, including encouragement and breaking down of barriers.

All seven characteristics are of course not predominant in all instances of OCC mission programs. For example, I know of many exceptions to the norm of Korean OCC leaders assuming responsibility in certain ministry settings, including in Korean-Japanese partnerships in planning and executing Love Sonata events. In general, however, these seven characteristics hold true of OCC mission ministries – positively, negatively, and otherwise.

Observations and Analyses

For the remainder of this section, I will offer some observations and analyses of why identifiably Korean traits characterize OCC's mission orientation and practice in the ways that they do. I will also dare to add some evaluative comments regarding the formation and the effects of such traits.

As noted in the study's first section, the suffering that Koreans have experienced in recent generations has cultivated a determination and capacity to endure hardship, as well as humility to serve. Such qualities come from the Holy Spirit's gracious work in lives, of course, but often the Spirit uses suffering to produce that kind of fruit.

Related are an exuberance, full-fledged passion, and open expression of emotion integral to Korean mission service. Prayers are offered intensely. Worship is often loud. Love Sonata events exhibit bright colors, paper airplanes, gifts of wreaths, and legions of smiling greeters with expressive welcoming signs.[98]

The strong Korean sense of calling arises from the experience of revival that has developed OCC and Korean churches in general. Pastor Ha and others have

---

98   For example, see the rolling home page for http://www.lovesonata.org/.

experienced God's powerful work, and there is a resulting sense of calling to share that experience with others. (There is the additional, supporting sense that God has blessed Korea in general, including economically, as part of Korea's divine calling by God through granting them revival.) Related to that revival-produced sense of calling is the historical sense of having been sandwiched between, and all too often oppressed by, Japan and China. Hence there is a deep, competitive desire to move out from under those two countries' large shadows, including by even surpassing them in service (as well as through serving them). Many Korean churches seem to have the sense that they are now the ones called to complete world evangelization. OCC's sense of calling fits into that same stream, historically cultivated by revival and by Sino-Japanese overshadowing.

In connection with the two contributing factors related to calling just sketched, two other interrelated Korean sets of sensibilities contribute to OCC's – like many other Korean churches' – subconscious compulsion to exhibit and to transmit Korean traits to others they serve in mission.[99] Thankfully such unwitting exporting is mitigated by the Korean and Spirit-produced humility, honoring of others, and servant hearts described above. Moreover, the universal tendency to colonize others culturally in mission service is a much discussed subject. With those caveats in mind, it is important to highlight these two additional sets of sensibilities.

One is a collective pride in Korean culture, including that many of its aspects are simply the world's best in various ways. The Korean script *Hangul* (한글), the fifteenth-century creation of which is now an official national holiday after having been commemorated since the 1920s, is celebrated as the world's simplest and most scientifically devised script. (Nationalistic efforts toward exclusively using *Hangul* and eliminating Chinese characters – and occasionally toward even purging all foreign influences from Korean language use in general – as well as favorable non-Korean assessments of *Hangul*[100] help to buttress Korean linguistic pride.[101]) As for cuisine, many Koreans not only simply prefer Korean food to other options but

---

99   I offer these comments with a sizeable measure of fear and trembling, aware that others (including U.S.-Americans) also export their own peculiar traits to others.

100   Several such assessments are assembled in "Quotes about Hangeul" on the Voluntary Agency Network of Korea website at http://korea.prkorea.com/wordpress/english/quote/quotes-about-hangeul/.

101   See, for example, the succinct study by Mark S. Lovmo, "Language Purism in Korea," available online at http://dokdo-research.com/gallery15.html

also consider it the most tasty and healthy.[102] Within interpersonal relationships, accepted protocols tied to age differences and Confucian hierarchical ranking are to be followed (regardless of contextual location) both out of unquestioned compulsion and out of preference over other alternatives.

Korean cultural pride is also based on an extensive list of Korean inventions and discoveries. In addition to *Hangul* is the world's first armored warship (the "turtle ship" or 거북선 (*geobukseon*)), the first movable type created two centuries prior to Gutenberg's invention, and all sorts of others in agriculture, architecture, astronomy, writing, printing, music, horology, ceramics, traditional medicine, military, mathematics, science, technology, traditional games, martial arts, sports, and various products.[103] Koreans are not boisterous about such matters, but there is a quiet assurance and pride in the factual accuracy of these monumental accomplishments.

Another set of sensibilities is related to Koreans' cultural homogeneity. At least one study baldly states, "The Korean people are the most homogeneous people on earth" despite foreign invasions and occupations, modern diasporas (due to both emigration and immigration, as noted earlier), and increasing percentages of international marriages.[104] While South Korea's international (particularly economic) rise has provided a Korean U.N. Secretary-General, Ban Ki-moon (2007-2016), globally recognized corporate brands, Korea's hosting of both the Summer (1988) and Winter (2018) Olympics, Korea's co-hosting of the FIFA World Cup (2002), and numerous internationally-known sports and pop-culture stars, cultural homogeneity remains a source of pride for many South Koreans.[105] The same can be said for the Korean Christian world, particularly regarding Christian mission. Koreans have assumed several positions of international leadership, and it is frequently noted that Korea now ranks second – behind only the United States – in sending out (Protestant) missionaries. Such growth and leadership supports a pride in cultural homogeneity.

---

102   Korean missionaries are notorious for eating Korean food, most Korean expatriates today have ample access to Korean groceries and restaurants, and many Korean restaurants cater to Korean tour groups.

103   The categories are from the Wikipedia "List of Korean inventions and discoveries" at https://en.wikipedia.org/wiki/List_of_Korean_inventions_and_discoveries.

104   "Demographics of South Korea," in *New World Encyclopedia*, available online at http://www.newworldencyclopedia.org/entry/Demographics_of_South_Korea.

105   Many accessible studies attest to this continuing pride in cultural homogeneity.

Onnuri Community Church provides a marvelous case study for examining the Korean character of its mission orientation. The Spirit's character fruit of love, joy, peace, patience, kindness, goodness, faithfulness, gentleness, and self-control is abundantly evident among the OCC pastoral and mission leadership, missionaries and supporting staff, and collaborating leaders and Christians in OCC's mission contexts. So is the Spirit's ministry fruit of conversions, church growth, spiritual maturing, villages rebuilt, immigrants and refugees served, and increased ministry partnerships. The Holy Spirit has been using and refining OCC's Korean qualities listed and analyzed above, including fervent prayer; a strong sense of calling; humility, sacrifice, and full-fledged passion in service; exuberant expression of emotion; and, hierarchical decision-making (tempered by leveled leadership structures and by the senior pastors' examples) regarding assignments for missionaries, pastors, and staff within OCC's overall matrix of mission ministry.

Furthermore, *Onnuri* Community Church – together with elements considered earlier in this study's nuanced discussion and caveats – exhibits a particular Korean sense of calling to be uniquely used by God to write the next (and final) chapter of Acts and to usher in God's final Kingdom. OCC's *Why Mission?* course, offered frequently throughout OCC campuses and networks, adapts the widely used *Perspectives on the World Christian Movement*[106] course by including the modern mission to *Chosun* (Korea) and the Acts 29 vision.[107] OCC's mission vision, winsomely inculcated by Pastor Ha Yong-jo, is a "Mosaic Vision" involving OCC, along with its collaborating ministries and churches, to ring out across the *onnuri* ("whole world") "the sound of God's heartfelt Love Sonata."[108]

With its particular historical background and traits, the Korean Onnuri Community Church is trusting God to use it to transform the whole world.

Opposition

For OCC, the primary and fundamental opposition it has faced in fulfilling its mission vision has been spiritual. That is a central reason why prayer has always

---

106   See http://www.perspectives.org/.
107   Compiled by Onnuri 2000 Mission Headquarters, *Why Mission?*. Seoul: Duranno Press, 2015.
108   Ha, 371-373.

permeated OCC's mission efforts and indeed its entire church life.[109] OCC's charismatic aspect frees people to pray for God's intervention against demonic forces, as well as to have seen exorcisms occur.[110] While Satanic and demonic opposition is of course not unique to OCC, explicitly noting it here is important for this study and for OCC.

Leaders' and missionaries' untimely deaths should be mentioned here. (Unexpected illnesses have also hindered mission efforts, but Ha Yong-jo's experience and testimony of God using his continual illnesses for good – particularly including expanding his vision for OCC[111]– turn that particular "opposition" into more of an ally.) In addition to Pastor Ha's death in 2011, since 2000 six OCC missionaries (plus one approved missionary in 1999) have died – three from illnesses and three from car accidents – including the widely known Samuel Kim, described earlier.[112]

What some might prefer labelling as a "barrier" has been the South Korean government's ban on travel to certain dangerous countries. In 2007, the ban was instituted for Somalia, Iraq, and Afghanistan following the 2004 beheading of a Korean Christian in Iraq and 2007 killings of two members of a Korean short-term mission team to Afghanistan.[113] As of late November 2015, three additional countries were on the travel ban list (Syria, Yemen, and Libya).[114] Different Christian leaders have discussed the pros and cons of the travel bans,[115] but in any

---

109   For example, not only do various prayer groups abound (including ones devoted to praying for missionaries), but musicians pray before and after worship services, as I have regularly witnessed (and photographed).

110   Pastor Ha testified about demons being cast out during his earlier days of ministry as well, in the 1970s before he went to England and well before OCC began. Ha, 68.

111   *Onnuri Community Church: The First 30 Years*, 284-286.

112   *Onnuri Community Church: The First 30 Years*, 277-280.

113   About the 2004 incident, see Jackie Spinner and Anthony Faiola, "S. Korean Is Beheaded in Iraq" Washington Post, June 23, 2004, available online at http://www.washingtonpost.com/wp-dyn/articles/A62068-2004Jun22.html. Reflections and discussions about the 2007 killings are in Sarah Pulliam, "In the Aftermath of a Kidnapping" *Christianity Today*, November 7, 2007, available online at http://www.christianitytoday.com/ct/2007/november/22.64.html?start=1. Regarding the 2007 travel ban, see Yoon Won-sup, "South Korea Bans Travel to Afghanistan" *The Korea Times*, August 1, 2007, available online at http://www.koreatimes.co.kr/www/nation/2017/05/113_7556.html.

114   Yeo Jun-suk, "Korea to reinforce travel bans on restricted countries" *The Korean Herald*, November 18, 2015, available online at http://www.koreaherald.com/view.php?ud=20151118001179.

115   Ruth Moon, "South Korea's Travel Bans a Blessing in Disguise for Missions" *Christianity Today*, October 1, 2013, available online at http://www.christianitytoday.com/ct/2013/october/south-koreas-travel-bans-lessing-in-disguise-for-missions.html.

case, OCC's direct mission efforts into these six countries – including Iraq, where in 2003 Samuel Kim had begun OCC's work – have been largely stymied.[116]

General Criticisms

OCC has also faced various criticisms, including missiological critiques that especially require attention here. One public criticism comes from the surrounding society toward Korean churches in general, since several prominent "Protestant leaders have been caught up in sensational scandals …, and as a result, people's attitudes toward Christian evangelicals have soured."[117] OCC has not been connected with any such scandal, but its megachurch status lumps it together as an object of much of the South Korean public's negative attitudes toward churches' perceived wealth, undue socio-political influence, and corruption.

In a direct connection with international mission efforts, the public's negativity gushed out during and immediately after the 2007 short-term mission team hostage crisis in Afghanistan, when widespread sympathy for the 23 hostages (two of whom were killed) became mixed with fury against "the Protestants' arrogant and blatant behavior" in going to such a dangerous region. The whole country was effectively taken hostage during the ordeal, raising accompanying questions about the South Korean government's possible ransom payments, as well as about Korean participation in the U.S.-led military intervention in the region.[118] Again, OCC

---

116   While OCC's "direct" efforts may have been "largely" stymied, relationships with others in those countries have enabled prayer and other means of involvement. As explained in the aforementioned and forthcoming "Reverse Migration Ministries from Korea: A Case Study of Onnuri Community Church's M Mission," OCC has strong connections with two Iraqi pastors in Erbil (northern Iraq) since their studies in Seoul and involvements with OCC. As a U.S.-American citizen I traveled in March 2017 to visit these pastors and their church on OCC's behalf. Also, the OCC Vision Church in Abu Dhabi supports the church in Erbil with prayer and finances.

117   Matthew Bell, "The biggest megachurch on Earth and South Korea's 'crisis of evangelism'" *PRI (Public Radio International)*, May 1, 2017. Available online at https://www.pri.org/stories/2017-05-01/biggest-megachurch-earth-facing-crisis-evangelism. For a summary of three recent scandals involving Korean megachurch pastors, see Sung-Gun Kim, "The Church Growth Movement: A Protestant Experience with the Rise of Megachurches," in Wonsuk Ma and Kyo Seong Ahn, eds., *Korean Church, God's Mission, Global Christianity.* Vol. 26, Regnum Edinburgh Centenary Series, eds., Knud Jørgensen, Kirsteen Kim, Wonsuk Ma, Tony Gray. Oxford: Regnum Books International, 2015, 134-135.

118   Choe Sang-hun, "Anger is Tempering Sympathy for South Korean Hostages" *New York Times*, August 3, 2007. Available online at http://www.nytimes.com/2007/08/03/world/asia/03korea.html?mcubz=0.

was not directly associated with this particular event,[119] but the general criticisms have necessarily forced fresh reconsideration of strategies (including regarding Muslim regions), attitudes, and wider implications.[120]

Missiological Criticisms

There have been at least four types of missiological criticisms leveled against OCC's mission efforts. One criticism - which some consider a matter of "evangelism" more than of "mission" per se - concerns OCC's intentional and expressed "tailored evangelism" approach, per Pastor Ha's own description.[121] In my extensive interviews with a wide cross-section of people about OCC (conducted inside and outside of OCC circles), one of the most blistering criticisms I have heard was about Pastor Ha's "business approach" to mission and evangelism. Essentially using marketing tools to attract people (so the critique goes), OCC has been able to gather large groups of similar-type people - often "sheep-stealing" them away from smaller local churches like a "supermarket" destroys small local shops - rather than relying on the Christian gospel to attract "whosoever will come." The criticism links with an unfavorable evaluation of OCC's instigation of "seeker-friendly" services that OCC began after sending a large contingent to visit Willow Creek Church in 1996 (as part of an extensive North American investigative tour).

Pastor Ha openly acknowledged that OCC indeed followed the model both of corporate marketing techniques[122] and of churches like Saddleback and Willow Creek that intentionally appeal to seekers.[123] Moreover, Pastor Ha and OCC have openly recounted their implementation and expansion of tailored evangelism conferences, have laid out "five stages of tailored evangelism," and have enthusiastically recommended other churches to follow the same course.[124]

In a specifically missiological way, Pastor Ha claimed Jesus's incarnation was a type of "tailored management" in order to relate to people, as were Jesus's "evangelistic principles":

119   Writing soon after the event, Pastor Ha noted the eventual fruit to come from the deaths: "This is the book of Acts. The death of one pastor and one laity will bring forth the fruit of the Gospel in Afghanistan, fifty to one hundred years from now." Ha, 146.
120   Pulliam.
121   Ha, 269-276, 356-357.
122   Ha, 269-270.
123   Ha, 265-267.
124   Ha, 265-267. Ha, 272-276; *Onnuri Community Church: The First 30 Years*, 156-171.

Jesus connected with the people and He customized His evangelistic effort according to the person he was talking to. The content of the Gospel never changed but his delivery and medium changed according to the person. In the same way, we must meet the people where they are at. Tailored evangelism focused on the needs of the individual and where they come from in terms of language, culture, and circumstance. When we are able to find that point of contact through which the Gospel can be shared, the individual naturally enters into the Gospel.[125]

Not all critics will be satisfied with OCC's testimonies of positive results or with their biblical-theological interpretation-application of Jesus's life and ministry. For its part, OCC has opted to see gospel fruit, as people "targeted" have continued to come to faith in Jesus Christ.

Despite OCC's tailoring its approach to people after listening to them and otherwise responsibly conducting its market research, a second criticism is that OCC missionaries and mission groups (especially short-term groups) do not listen to others' advice or input. Several instances have been conveyed to me of OCC groups proceeding in a manner that they were convinced was best and according to God's leading, but that indigenous observers or other more experienced expatriate missionaries in the situation saw as presumptuous and in effect harmful. The size and financial resources of most OCC groups only exacerbate the resulting problems, so it is claimed.

My own assessment of this criticism is necessarily multifaceted, nuanced, and tentative. For one, OCC missionaries and mission groups are not the only ones that do not - and sometimes cannot - hear or understand the other people among whom they minister. Related is the reality that such cross-cultural understanding takes both experience and time, and most often short-term mission groups have neither. Another factor relates to the twin mitigating factors of the Korean mission movement's relative inexperience and the combined Korean cultural homogeneity and pride that characterize many Korean missionaries and mission groups, as discussed earlier. Finally, a much more sanguine aspect is that, while I concur with the criticism in various instances, I know many OCC missionaries, pastors, mission

---

125   Ha, 271. The English translation has been left as is.

elders, staff, and members that exhibit deep cross-cultural sensibilities as well as a consistent track record of listening to others' input and advice in conducting cross-cultural mission work.

A third type of criticism is of an expressly biblical-theological nature and is associated with OCC's megachurch, "big tent" acceptance of a wide range of ministries. Some who know OCC well wish there were a more thoroughly articulated and agreed-upon theological mission vision, rather than just the cryptic "Acts 29" and "2000/10000" phrases. Other critics, including those coming from a Reformed traditional framework, theologically question OCC's charismatic traits in mission, including speaking in tongues, strategic prayer that targets demonic powers, and prayer walks. OCC has never felt the need to justify the charismatic expressions that are vital parts of its life and mission efforts, but instead gladly embraces the free and vibrant work of the Spirit in and through its ministries - based as well on Pastor Ha's understanding and teaching of the Book of Acts underlying OCC's pervasive Acts 29 vision.

The more widespread and strident biblical-theological criticisms I have heard are directed at OCC's connection with the Korea Israel Bible Institute (KIBI).[126] KIBI now has its own structures and programs that operate quite independently of OCC, including international networks with a strong base in the U.S.[127] Even so, OCC's involvements in Israel-focused ministries began in 1990, and those initiatives are what developed into KIBI. Also, OCC continues to participate in KIBI's ministries by supplying office space, hosting seminars, and attending high-profile events, particularly the "Shalom Yerushalayim Cultural Festival" held in the U.S.[128] KIBI's multi-faceted ministries include Bible teaching, prayer networks, and support of worldwide Jews settling in the modern state of Israel. The OCC-KIBI relationship is not the closest and may be even a bit uneasy; one cannot find KIBI links on the OCC website, for example, and KIBI prayer needs are not among those publicized in OCC networks the way other ministries' are. Even so, the association has been strong in many observers' minds, especially

---

126   See the KIBI website at http://kibi.or.kr; *Onnuri Community Church: The First 30 Years*, 241-247.

127   See the KIBI America website at http://www.kibiamerica.org/.

128   See the event's web page at http://www.kibiamerica.org/shalom-jerusalem.

through highly publicized events such as the 2005 Jerusalem Peace March that CGNTV broadcast through its satellite network.[129]

Criticisms first object on biblical-theological grounds to KIBI's emphases, disagreeing with its dispensational framework of strongly separating Israel and the Church. Second, socio-political criticisms focus on what increasing Jewish settlers in modern-day Israel mean for Palestinians who are displaced, as well as for the entire region's peace and stability.[130] Presently, the OCC-KIBI relationship is ever-developing and under review.

The fourth type of criticism concerns mission strategy. In particular, OCC has its own missionary sending structure, Tyrannus International Mission (TIM).[131] At the foundation of Pastor Ha's vision for OCC, TIM and Duranno Press - which essentially share the same name from Acts 19 - were OCC's twin publishing and personnel outreach arms.[132] TIM is thus interwoven into the very fabric of OCC's life and ministry. Hence within OCC's framework, TIM is not simply what is criticized: a mission "sodality" run by the "modality" Onnuri Community Church, an all-encompassing megachurch trying to do the job of all others including those with special expertise.

OCC has resisted suggestions that it should not have its own mission sodality. For its part, OCC actively cooperates with many sodalities, with approximately half of its current 900 missionaries serving with a wide range of mission agencies other than TIM. Hence OCC does not simply fund and otherwise operate TIM as its own mission agency at the total expense of all others. The deeper apologetic - in tandem with TIM's role within OCC's DNA - is how operating TIM keeps OCC mission-focused. As is the case with OCC's other organizations, the Senior Pastor is the official head and hence responsible for TIM's mission functions, including missionary training, deployment, and care. That active operation of TIM helps to

---

129   A synopsis published soon after that 2005 event is available on the U.S.-CGNTV website, "Shalom, Jerusalem! Shalam, Palestine!" Available online at http://us.cgntv.net/sub.asp?mode=&idx=41&Gubun=0605&gotopage=41&Search_type=&search_andOr=&search_Keyword=.

130   I share both of these criticisms. I also appreciate KIBI's evangelistic emphasis, as well as its strong focus on Jesus's Second Coming.

131   A helpful English overview of TIM is Meesaeng Lee Choi, "Tyrannus International Mission America," in George Thomas Kurian and Mark A. Lamport, eds., *Encyclopedia of Christianity in the United States*, Vol. 5. Lanham, Maryland: Rowman & Littlefield, 2016, 2346-2347; see the TIM website at http://tim.or.kr.

132   See, for example, Pastor Ha's early budding thought about Duranno in Ha, 81-82.

keep a mission orientation at the center of OCC's life and ministries.[133] OCC's maintaining its own mission sodality also reflects many of the early influences given through Pastor Ha's involvements in England with WEC and OMF,[134] as well as Missionary Samuel Kim's Christian and Missionary Alliance affiliation.

It should come as no surprise that OCC, even though widely appreciated and remarkably scandal-free, as a mission-oriented megachurch would have had various criticisms directed its way. It should also be no surprise that OCC has remained undeterred in its passion to see the whole world, the *onnuri*, blessed through its wide-sweeping programs and initiatives. Despite all types of opposition, God's Spirit and OCC's mission vision compel OCC to press ever onward.

A "Missional Megachurch"?

OOC has always understood itself to be missional. Moreover, it is constantly aiming to become more missional, or at least to refine its missional character. Particularly under Senior Pastor Lee Jae-hoon's recent leadership, OCC has held a number of seminars, conferences, and study sessions on the theme of "missional church," aimed at public audiences and particularly at OCC pastoral training.[135]

In English-language circles and publications, discussions about the relationship between "missional" and "megachurch" have abounded over the last ten years. The separate tracks of "Missional Church" discussions[136] and "Megachurch" studies,[137] each of which had gained traction in the mid-1990s,[138] intersected

---

133   Current OCC Mission 2000 Head Pastor Kim Hong-joo has helpfully articulated this rationale in discussions he and I have had.

134   Ha, 77-78, 84-85.

135   As just two examples in which I have personally participated, Michael Frost ("one of the leading voices in the missional church movement," as noted on the "Missional Church Network" website at http://missionalchurchnetwork.com/category/michael-frost/), was the featured speaker at the annual OCC pastors retreat in February, 2016; and, "missional church" was the theme of the June, 2017 Vision Conference for all OCC Vision Church pastors.

136   See "History of Missional Church" on the "Missional Church Network" website at http://missionalchurchnetwork.com/history-of-missional-church/.

137   These research efforts were spearheaded by Scott Thumma of the Hartford Institute for Religion Research – see http://www.hartfordinstitute.org/megachurch/megachurches_research.html; and, Warren Bird of the Dallas-based church resource center Leadership Network – see http://leadnet.org/.

138   See, for example, Philip Yancey, "Why I Don't Go to a Megachurch" *Christianity Today*, May 20, 1996, available online at http://www.christianitytoday.com/ct/1996/may20/6t6080.html.

about ten years ago with a flurry of articles and blogposts discussing the topic of "Missional Megachurch."[139] Some analysts have been positive about examples they have studied.[140] Some claim that megachurches and other churches face essentially the same challenges, hence all churches should be encouraged in their faithfulness and ministries.[141] Others have accused megachurches of stealing members from other churches,[142] while even other critics have argued that "Any mega-trended and mega-minded churches that have the tendencies associated with the megachurch cannot be missional,"[143] essentially making the phrase "missional megachurch" an oxymoron. Even if the more public spirited discussions may have abated, the same questions and impressions are ongoing.

As for discussions in Korean, English-language "missional church" publications were introduced starting in 2002. Since then, translations and Korean-

---

139   See, for example, the following online (except the second) resources, listed here in chronological order of appearance: Brother Maynard, "More Thoughts on Megachurch & Missional Church," on "Subversive Influence," October 7, 2005, http://subversiveinfluence. com/2005/10/more-thoughts-on-megachurch-missional-church/; Mark Driscoll, *Confessions of a Reformission Rev.: Hard Lessons from an Emerging Missional Church.* Leadership Network Innovation Series. Grand Rapids, Michigan: Zondervan, 2006; Ed Stetzer, "Missional Churches and Mega Churches," on "The Exchange," March 20, 2008, http://www.christianitytoday.com/edstetzer/2008/march/missional-churches-and-mega-churches.html; David Fitch, "What is Missional? – Can a Mega Church Be Missional?" on "Missio Alliance," June 3, 2008, http://www.missioalliance.org/what-is-missional-can-a-mega-church-be-missional/; Andy Rowell, "Following Dan Kimball's Missional vs. Megachurch conversation," on "Church Leadership Conversations," December 6, 2008, http://www.andyrowell.net/andy_rowell/2008/12/following-dan-kimballs-missional-vs-megachurch-conversation.html; J. R. Woodward, "Can the Mega Church be Missional?" October 9, 2009, http://jrwoodward.net/2009/10/can-the-mega-church-be-missional/.

140   Ed Stetzer has perhaps been the most prominent analyst who has cited positive examples of megachurches and argued for their acceptance into the necessarily varied landscape of types of churches. See, for example, the conclusion of Stetzer's five-part online series "Can Mega Be Missional? Part V: Where Do We Go From Here?" on "The Exchange, September 24, 2012, http://www.christianitytoday.com/edstetzer/2012/september/can-mega-be-missional-part-v-where-do-we-go-from-here.html.

141   Mike Breen, "Can Mega Be Missional?" on the "Verge Network" website at https://www.vergenetwork.org/2012/12/11/can-mega-be-missional/.

142   David Fitch, "Mega Churches Steal Sheep: My Ongoing Debate With Ed Stetzer," on the "Missio Alliance" website, February 26, 2013, http://www.missioalliance.org/mega-churches-steal-sheep-my-ongoing-debate-with-ed-stetzer/.

143   C. J. P. Niemandt and Y. Lee, "A Korean Perspective on Megachurches as Missional Churches" *Verbum et Ecclesia* 36(1), Art. #1421, 2015, 8, http://dx.doi.org/10.4102/ve.v36i1.1421.

initiated discussions have abounded.[144] Even so, after years of extensive discussions in Korea and diaspora Korean churches worldwide, "The concept of missional church remains unclear in the Korean church and so it is still in the process of development and testing."[145]

Open discussions in Korea about megachurches have been basically nonexistent due to the sensitivity of the topic. One exception was the Korean Global Mission Leadership Forum, held in November 2015 and co-hosted by OCC. The KGMLF resulted in a book of the forum's papers (in English and Korean) entitled *Megachurch Accountability in Missions*,[146] as well as a CGNTV panel discussion in its "Global Talk" series, "Megachurches and Mission."[147] Hence insofar as "missional megachurch" is a Korean topic, OCC is spearheading the effort.

"Missional Church"

What do these discussions mean for OCC being a "missional megachurch"? First is to note that the "missional church" discussions arose and have developed in Western (and more particularly English-speaking) contexts in the wake of Lesslie Newbigen's observations about the Western Church/churches. While Newbigen's instincts and insights were shaped by his experience in India, the "missional church" discussions grew out of Newbigen's writings about "The Church's" need to be "missional" in the West. Hence a primary impetus for missional church thinking, publications, and discussions has focused – usually unwittingly, especially initially – on the Post-Christendom Western-Anglo Church's/churches' need to understand itself/themselves as having been sent into mission in its/their own Western-Anglo contexts.[148]

---

144   An excellent and detailed account is in Sung-kon Park, "Missional Ecclesiology: Missionary Encounters between the Presbyterian Church of Korea (*Tonghap*) and Protestant Churches in the Czech Republic and Slovakia," PhD Thesis, Károli Gáspár Reformed University, Budapest, 2017, 24-29, available online at http://corvina.kre.hu:8080/phd/Park_Sun_Kong_Thesis.pdf.

145   Park, 33, 38.

146   Jinbong Kim et al, eds., *Megachurch Accountability in Missions: Critical Assessment through Global Case Studies*. Pasadena, CA: William Carey Library, 2016. The Korean version was published by Duranno Press.

147   "Global Talk" Panel Discussion on CGN-TV, "Megachurches and Mission," November, 2015, available online at m.cgntv.net/player.cgn?v=178101.

148   See again "History of Missional Church" on the (North American) "Missional Church Network" website at http://missionalchurchnetwork.com/history-of-missional-church/.

This Western-Anglo contextual seedbed for missional church understandings has thus largely shaped the developing discussions by instincts and concerns particular to Western-Anglo Christianity(ies). The "Post-Christendom" framework has been the single largest driving force for the discussions. In the U.K. and Anglo-Commonwealth settings (most especially Australia), that framework has developed together with the decolonization of the British Empire and reverse migration of non-Anglos into Britain and Anglo-Commonwealth countries; the U.S. setting has been the gradual breakdown of persistent White-Protestant socio-political hegemony since the 1960s Civil Rights Movement and Immigration and Naturalization Act of 1965. How to live as Christian communities absent the socio-political-racial stability and homogeneity once comfortably enjoyed has in large part driven missional church discussions.

Theologically, the English-language missional church movement has necessarily used (including as foils) inherited Western-Anglo categories, e.g., systematic and historical theological labels, to carry out its discussions. The centrally important notion of *missio Dei* had come into mid-twentieth-century focus amid the post-World Wars European malaise and Western missionary movement's crisis following Communist China's expulsion of foreign agents. Mission leaders had indeed come to realize that mission was fundamentally the universal God's mission and not that of the (Western) Church – a realization that crystallized and was articulated in Euro-tribal linguistic-conceptualizations. As for historical labels, the "Post-Christendom" category presupposes a basic three-fold "Pre-/Christendom/Post-progression" wedded to an overall Greco-Roman Imperial/Western European history.

Moreover, the biblical foundations of such central missional church concerns as ecclesiology and the Christian gospel are inexorably intertwined with European Protestant instincts and parameters. That is not to say that such categories do not have at least some measure of wider and even universal applicability. It is to point out, however, that universal Christian history is much broader than what occurred in the Greco-Roman Empire, Europe, and their extensions, as well as that biblical understandings of God's people and the Good News about Jesus are not confined to Euro-tribal-Reformation notions and formulations.

In more general and striking terms, the "missional church" discussion has been WEIRD, i.e., it has developed within "Western, Educated, Industrialized, Rich and Democratic [and Anglo] societies" that are in fact a "particularly thin, and rather unusual, slice of humanity" and "are particularly unusual [and] frequent outliers" in comparison to the rest of the world.[149] Despite this "weird," minority character of its formative context, the missional church discussion's widespread dissemination into different but socio-politically, economically, religiously, and now electronically related contexts – including South Korea – has enabled even the possibility, and necessity, of raising the important question about OCC's "missional megachurch" character.

That enablement was not because substantial discussions about related matters were not already occurring. In fact, prior to importing "missional church" discussions and terminology, Korean Christian leaders were very much discussing "the missionary nature of the church, the society, and the missionary structure of the church," including by using the latest Western ecclesiological writings.[150] However, the entrance of "missional church" discussions into Korean linguistic circles stimulated further thinking but also, not surprisingly, brought on unwanted confusion. For example, as we will consider further below, the fact that the same Korean word (seongyojeok, 선교적) has been used for both "missional" and "missionary" in connection with "church" (gyohoe, 교회) has contributed to vague and misplaced emphases.[151] Therefore, caution should be exercised when analyzing the "missional" character of "megachurches" in non-Western-Anglo contexts, since doing so inevitably encounters such perils as predominantly using Western-Anglo sources[152] or dichotomous, "either-or" evaluative approaches.[153]

---

149   Joe Henrich, Steven J. Heine, and Ara Norenzayan, "The Weirdest People in the World?" (May 7, 2010). RatSWD Working Paper No. 139. Available online at http://dx.doi.org/10.2139/ssrn.1601785.

150   Park, 29-31.

151   Park, 38.

152   Genevieve Lerina James, "Mission and Three South African Metropolitan Megachurches: Middle-Class Masses in Search of Mammon?" in Beate Fagerli et al, eds., *A Learning Missional Church: Reflections from Young Missiologists*. Regnum Edinburgh Centenary Series. Oxford: Regnum Books International and Eugene, Oregon: Wipf & Stock Publishers, 2012, 171-184.

153   Niemandt and Lee.

"Megachurch"

Similarly, discussions of "megachurches" have arisen in even more "weird" U.S.-Anglo contexts, frequently focusing on big money,[154] size,[155] or various problems.[156] Note as well that the word "megachurch," its accepted definition of at least 2,000 weekly attendees,[157] and the focus of its research all have Anglo-U.S. origins. The combined realities of the Western-Anglo origins of both the "missional church" and "megachurch" discussions, as well as of the resulting "missional megachurch" discussion, should give further pause in approaching the non-Western-Anglo, Korean *Onnuri* Community Church.

This Discussion

Even so, before jettisoning this discussion about OCC and its possible "missional megachurch" character due to apparently total contextual discontinuity, we must account for two additional factors. One factor, to which earlier comments already alluded, is that contextual particularity does not necessarily imply wider discontinuity. Just because the "missional church," "megachurch," and "missional megachurch" discussions began and developed in "weird"-Anglo circles does not therefore mean their total irrelevance to OCC and its Korean context. Indeed, along with the significance that all types of Christians give to such central concerns as God's people and the Good News of Jesus, the internationally-related socio-political, economic, and religious dynamics involved with "missional" and "megachurch" ideas and concerns very much imply relevance beyond the limited "weird"-Anglo set of contexts.

---

154   A relatively early analysis was by Luisa Kroll, "Megachurches, Megabusinesses" *Forbes*, September 17, 2003, available online at https://www.forbes.com/2003/09/17/cz_lk_0917megachurch.html.

155   "More Americans Flock to Mega-Churches," *ABC News*, available online at http://abcnews.go.com/US/story?id=93111&page=1; Jesse Bogan, "America's Biggest Megachurches" *Forbes*, June 26, 2009, available online at https://www.forbes.com/2009/06/26/americas-biggest-megachurches-business-megachurches.html.

156   Ruth Graham, "How a Megachurch Melts Down," *The Atlantic*, November 7, 2014, available online at https://www.theatlantic.com/national/archive/2014/11/houston-mark-driscoll-megachurch-meltdown/382487/.

157   "Megachurch Definition," Hartford Institute for Religion Research, available online at http://hirr.hartsem.edu/megachurch/definition.html.

Furthermore, South Korea and OCC have intentionally taken on extra-Korean features, including specifically Western-Anglo features. The U.S. role in twentieth-century Korea (including post-Korean War South Korea) has been particularly significant, ranging from early U.S. missionaries' influences to U.S. military intervention to the U.S.-ROK political alliance to varied U.S.-Korean socio-economic interchanges. OCC has intentionally imbibed U.S./U.K.-Anglo theological and ecclesiological elements, including through Pastor Ha's early-1980s sojourn in England, Pastor Lee's extensive periods of study and pastoring in the U.S., the church leaders' 1996 investigative trip to the U.S., and many OCC associate and assistant pastors having done at least parts of their formal theological studies in the U.S. The early and continuing prominence given to OCC's English ministry (OEM),[158] OCC using English in much of its branding and publicity,[159] and a steady stream of Anglo guest speakers[160] are only a few of the many evidences of OCC's clearly Anglo features. OCC is definitely Korean, and there are other international features (especially Japanese, as well as Chinese) that are on prominent display, but for the purposes of this discussion the importance of Anglo-related factors must not be discounted.

An additional, obvious consideration is that this is an English-language discussion, carrying along all sorts of non-Korean and subliminal freight, be it psychological, theological, or otherwise. At this point in this discussion, then, I am suspending any sort of definitive judgment as to OCC's "missional megachurch" character. On the one hand, OCC assuredly is a "missional megachurch." As I claimed at the outset, "OCC is perhaps the most mission-oriented church that I know"; and, by common consent OCC (including in its own self-understanding) is a megachurch. On the other hand, in its Korean capacity OCC has never experienced a "Christendom" and thus is not striving for any sort of "Post-Christendom" type of "missional" character per se; and, while OCC undoubtedly has a large corporate *modus operandi* similar to that of U.S. megachurches, OCC's ethos also undoubtedly and distinctively resembles a Korean conglomerate or *chaebol* (財閥, 재벌) "that does not operate along the lines of its European and Anglo-American

---

158   The only non-Korean Sunday worship service held in the main sanctuary at OCC's main Seobinggo campus is the 4:00 pm English service.

159   Note the ubiquitous "Onnuri Community Church" English-language logo, as well as the English-language annual church slogan alongside the Korean (for 2017, "Turn Back to God and Live"), e.g., on the church website at http://www.onnuri.org/.

160   Whether personally or via CGNTV.

counterparts."[161] Whether or not to describe OCC's mission orientation in terms of its being a "missional megachurch" is thus a matter better left undecided – at least for now in this English-language discussion.

We are not, however, left in frustrating limbo in analyzing OCC's mission orientation. Instead, we are redirected to OCC's particular setting in which it has developed: its historical context of suffering, revivals, economy, and diaspora; its particular features of the Spirit, leadership, inherent "megachurch" character, and *onnuri* disposition; and, aspects and implications of OCC being Korean. Also, as we recall the various forms of opposition that OCC has faced, as well as keep in mind the nuanced and (at least for now) inconclusive matter of OCC being termed a "missional megachurch," we can now appropriately consider the important missiological topic of how "missional" and "missions" figure into OCC's mission orientation.

"Missional" and "Missions"

Among the various challenges OCC has faced in its mission orientation, none requires more careful attention and missiological acumen than the challenge of integrating its "missional" and "missions" heritages. In approaching this particular topic, we must remember the just-discussed caveats of, first, the inherent foreignness of at least certain aspects of the "missional church" discussion (as well as research and discussions about "megachurch"), as well as the ever-developing nature of that discussion (both in English and in Korean).[162] In any case, the matter before us now concerns the following: under Pastor Ha Yong-jo's leadership, OCC was born and developed as both "missional" as a caring, Spirit-filled community that served surrounding communities holistically (including evangelistically), as well as decidedly devoted to a more "traditional"[163] form of "missions" centered on

---

161   David Murillo and Yun-dal Sung, "Understanding Korean Capitalism: *Chaebols* and their Corporate Governance," ESADEgeo-Center for Global Economy and Geopolitics, Ramon Llull University, Position Paper 33, September 2013, available online at https://www.google.com/url?sa=t&rct=j&q=&esrc= s&source=web&cd=1&cad=rja&uact=8&ved=0ahUKEwj4mJHQlN7UAhVEbz4K 0ahUKEwj4mJHQlN7UAhVEbz4KHbPRAuEQFggoMAA&url=http%3A%2F%2Fwww. esadegeo.com%2Fdownload%2FPR_PositionPapers%2F43%2FficPDF_ ENG%2F201309%2520Chaebols_Murillo_Sung_EN.pdf&usg=AFQjCNHO AFQjCNHOcdcRqncSn9zqmjSc6YEpoAFQjCNHOcdcRqncSn9zqmjSc6YEpo3a4hw.

162   See, for example, "What is Missional?" on the Missional Church Network website at http://missionalchurchnetwork.com/what-is-missional/.

163   I am using "traditional" in the sense of the "Modern Missions Movement" associated with European migration throughout the world, beginning about half a millennium ago.

sending out missionaries. Now under Pastor Lee Jae-hoon's leadership, OCC is seeking to weave together more seamlessly these two strands. This attempt presents a significant, multifaceted challenge.

The Challenge

What, more precisely, is the nature of this challenge? One crucial point mentioned earlier is the struggle presented by dealing with this matter *in Korean*. As already noted, "missionary church" and "missional church" are both translated as *seongyojeok gyohoe* (선교적 교회). An essential component of English-language "missional church" discussions is the distinction between the activist connotations of "missionary" and the combined theocentric and "sentness" thrusts of the term "missional." Using the same Korean expression for both English phrases risks collapsing the important distinction involved. Furthermore, since *seongyojeok* has carried an action-oriented meaning akin to "missionary church," the "missional church" discussion has tended to emphasize the practical outreach activities of the church – an emphasis quite different from the English-language intent.[164] Especially since Pastor Lee is an astute scholar, OCC mission leaders should be able to work through this linguistic vagueness and confusion.

Even so, understanding and dealing with OCC's "'missional' and 'missions'" challenge is compounded when conducted – as it of course must be – in Korean.

Beyond the linguistic subtleties involved, the mixed character of OCC's mission orientation is apparent in its self-description as "being focused on local and overseas missions as well as ["missional"] involvement in society throughout the [Korean] peninsula." That same varied character is evident in the five ministry traits OCC has highlighted in explaining its growth: "1) Bible-based; 2) Gospel-centered; 3) Missions-focused; 4) Compassionate; 5) Cultivating a Christ-cultured church. With this approach, Onnuri has grown [even more] since it introduced its Acts 29 vision in 2003."[165] These five ministry traits were then elucidated by Pastor Lee (as Pastor Ha's still new successor), who explained to church members OCC's forward-looking "Vision and Challenge" by using the combined metaphors

---

164   Park, 38-39.

165   *Onnuri Community Church: The First 30 Years*, 49-50.

of "Three Anchors and Five Sails."[166] Here, then, are Pastor Lee's descriptions of OCC's foundational "anchors" that "tie it to its core traditions and values":

- Anchor #1 – "Spirit-led missions" involving numerous missionaries and "monetary contributions to missions [that] surpass other churches."

- Anchor #2 – Spirit-instilled "free and creative development," meaning that "change should be a part of a church's tradition and standards."

- Anchor #3 – "… a community of humility and respect. Pastor Ha emphasized that Onnuri, as a multi-site church, … is unified as a whole."

Next are the five "sails" or principles to "'absorb' or use the hurdles and challenges" when "the Holy Spirit may allow difficulties to come our way, such as external changes or criticisms by those outside of the church":

- Sail #1 – "… better mid- to long-term plans for reaching out to [unreached] tribes and regions," for example plans for supporting missionaries through spiritual training resources like CGNTV.

- Sail #2 – "… organic and fundamental campus churches" that "will succeed as a community focused on its members' spiritual growth and the supporting programs."

- Sail #3 – "… domestic evangelization and raising the next generation within the Church…. As much as we focus on doing missions around the world, we need to place the same emphasis and invest our time and resources to reach the next generation."

- Sail #4 – "… reaching out to North Korea through social justice missions with the ultimate goal of achieving the reunification of the Korean peninsula."

- Sail #5 – "… your dedication and support for the Church. In order to expand God's Kingdom, we must be able to overcome the world by allowing Christ to sanctify us."

Finally, leading into OCC's 30-year anniversary commemoration events in September-October, 2015, Pastor Lee shared his updated vision for OCC's future, which was formally adopted by OCC and explained as follows:

---

166   Onnuri Community Church: The First 30 Years, 51-56. The quotations that follow are from these pages.

Christ obeyed the call to come to earth, which was full of sin, subject himself to humiliation, and be the ultimate sacrifice by being nailed to the Cross. The Book of Acts is a track record of people who became 'fools for Christ' by obeying God's call and gave up all their worldly possessions. It contains historical evidence of the actions taken by the apostles who chose to be 'fools for Christ'. With the Onnuri community transforming into 'fools for Christ', we will be able to carry out Onnuri's new '3 Anchors & 5 sails' vision.[167]

This latest "Fools for Christ" vision through Pastor Lee builds on the "Acts 29" vision declared by Pastor Ha in 2003, which filled out the "2000/10000" vision he declared in 1994. These three pithy phrases are the most all-encompassing and widely disseminated expressions of OCC's mission orientation throughout its now 32-year history.[168] They also embody the mixed meanings of "missional" and "missions" that OCC seeks to integrate.

facet #1

One important aspect of the challenge is one that Evangelicals have been discussing since the beginning of the Lausanne Movement in 1974, namely the prioritized relationship between evangelism and social ministry.[169] Over the past two years I have seen this topic arise on numerous occasions and in a variety of settings, public and private. Several times, OCC mission leaders have expressed the need to keep evangelism the top priority, with social ("missional") ministry an important but secondary means to facilitate evangelism. All indications suggest that varying viewpoints will persist among OCC mission leaders.

Practical implications for OCC's mission programs especially include budget allocations as well as personnel assignments, especially for TIM's approximately 450 missionaries. TIM's most recent overall focus has been on

---

167   *Onnuri Community Church: The First 30 Years*, 58.

168   I examined OCC's preference for such concise phrases in expressing its mission vision in a presentation, "Lengthy Documents or Pithy Phrases? Onnuri Community Church's Vision for Mission," to the Central and Eastern European Association of Mission Studies, Osijek, Croatia, February, 2017.

169   See, for example, the 1982 Lausanne Occasional Paper 21: "LOP 21: Evangelism and Social Responsibility: An Evangelical Commitment," available online at https://www.lausanne.org/content/lop/lop-21.

facilitating Church-Planting Movements (CPM), including encouraging Insider Movements (IM) when appropriate. At the same time, some TIM missionaries are being assigned to work with Onnuri's M Mission among foreign migrant workers in Ansan City, in the southwestern part of the Greater Seoul Metropolitan area. Other TIM missionaries serve in a variety of capacities throughout Asia and beyond, a few in a recently approved initiative to serve Middle Eastern refugees through computer training and related evangelistic outreach. More Onnuri-wide mission allocations will affect relative support for Better World (OCC's NGO), BEE, CGNTV, and other ministries not fully operated by OCC.

facet #2

Another aspect of this "'missional' and 'missions'" challenge is the ongoing nature of the "2000/10000" vision. When Pastor Ha declared this vision in 1994, the effect was stunning and electric: How on earth could a church of around 7,000 members send out 2,000 missionaries by the year 2010, as well as raise up 10,000 lay mission leaders? Understood by many as God's revealed vision for OCC, the church grew at an astonishing rate, ministries devoted to the Holy Spirit and prayer became even more vibrant and focused on sending missionaries, 15 unreached people groups were adopted between 1996 and 1999, and OCC's mission headquarters was named "Mission 2000." The vision has had a galvanizing effect for numerous OCC mission prayer groups, prayer letter teams, and all of OCC through the coordinating efforts of the Mission 2000 office.[170]

What is the current status of this "2000 Vision"? First, somehow the 2010 target date was lost or recalibrated. Since the cumulative total of missionaries sent out should soon reach 2,000, one suggestion (not yet widely disseminated or discussed) has been to refocus and enlarge the "2000 Vision" by aiming toward sending out 2,000 currently active missionaries rather than cumulatively.

Whether or not that decision is reached, the 2003 promulgation of the permeating "Acts 29" vision (and more recent "Fools for Christ" vision) has effectively decentralized – or at least clouded over the focus on – the "missions"-natured "2000 Vision." Related factors contributing to the slight fading of OCC's central focus on sending missionaries could have been the after-effect of the AD

---

170   *Onnuri Community Church: The First 30 Years*, 228-231. The "10000" part of the vision has been reinterpreted to mean every church member being involved in sending the 2,000 missionaries through financial support, prayer, and other involvements.

2000 & Beyond Movement, the goal of which was to see "A Church for Every People and the Gospel for Every Person by the Year 2000"[171] (as well as Jesus not having returned in the year A.D. 2000 as many had expected); and, the beginnings, growth, and publicity surrounding such international OCC ministries as CGNTV,[172] Love Sonata, and (while not as publicized) Better World.[173]

Another basic question concerns what type of "vision" that the "2000 Vision" has cultivated. Insofar as OCC sending out 2,000 missionaries was a heavenly "vision" that God revealed to Pastor Ha (as believed by many), the "2000 'Vision'" has been a target that OCC has been compelled and obligated to reach. Organizationally speaking, the "2000 Vision" has focused energies on what might more properly be called a "means" or "objective" to the envisioned fruit that should come from missionaries' labors, be they more Christian believers, churches, or otherwise. In that sense, the "2000 Vision" has had a limiting effect on OCC's vision for God's work in the world, including compared to the more goal-oriented "Better World" vision that OCC's NGO conveys.

facet #3

In addition to the contributions to OCC's "'missional' and "missions'" challenge that these first two facets of social-evangelistic priorities and "2000 Vision" make, another facet connects with the ever-developing nature of "missional" discussions described earlier. In short, OCC pastors and mission leaders – not to mention the wider membership – are regularly reading, hearing, participating in, and adding their own understandings to discussions about "missional church," or "*seongyojeok gyohoe*" (선교적 교회). As requested, I added some of my thoughts on the matter at OCC's recent 2017 Vision Conference held for OCC's worldwide Vision Church pastors. I gave a historically-oriented presentation on missional church, and on OCC, as a "Reactive/Reforming Movement, Preserving/ Continuing Movement, and Proactive / Innovative Movement."[174] While I received appreciative feedback, my comments added to the massive amount of information that OCC leaders continue to process about what it means to lead a "missional church," while continuing a "missions" (missionary-sending) emphasis, in their OCC capacities.

---

171   See the "AD2000 & Beyond Movement" website at http://www.ad2000.org/.

172   *Onnuri Community Church: The First 30 Years*, 211-215.

173   *Onnuri Community Church: The First 30 Years*, 211-215, 259-269, 321-328.

174   "Missional Church," International Vision Church Conference, Irvine, CA, May, 2017.

Having inherited a wide-ranging array of "missional" and "missions" programs and emphases from the Pastor Ha Yong-jo era up through 2011, the Pastor Lee Jae-hoon era of OCC – per the aforementioned second "anchor" of Spirit-instilled "free and creative development" – is continually adjusting, all the while maintaining, OCC's "missional" and "missions" emphases. On the church website, OCC's expressly stated "mission work" (*seongyowa sayeog*, 선교와 사역) begins with reaching "all peoples" (*modeun minjog*, 모든 민족) as stated in Matthew 28:19 and as carried out according to OCC's "2000 Vision." OCC's five mission organizations or "agencies" are then listed: Mission 2000 (headquarters), TIM (Tyrannus International Mission), Acts 29 Vision Village Training Center, M Mission, and Better World. (Other OCC-related mission organizations, such as BEE and CGNTV, are not listed due to their having a separate organizational structure.) Next are ministries listed under the "Acts 29" heading, namely Acts 29 campuses and Vision Churches, Christian Medical Network, and Love Sonata.[175] Continuity and change are evident, the latter with the increased emphases on M Mission and Better World.

The M Mission[176] in particular pushes OCC toward integrating "missional" and "missions" emphases. Ministering to immigrants in South Korea – particularly manual laborers but also students, businesspeople, and spouses of Koreans – is necessarily holistic, one hallmark of "missional" ministries. Legal, employment, financial, educational, family, literacy, and a host of other issues arise for immigrants that the M Mission addresses, along with conducting evangelistic and church-focused ministries. Furthermore, M mission efforts take place in South Korea: these efforts are "Doing Missions in the Homeland."[177] Insofar as "traditional" or modern "missions" have involved sending missionaries to other countries, OCC's assignment of TIM missionaries to serve among M Mission ministries begs the question of their "missionary" status in a manner that opens up new avenues for integrating "missional" and "missions" topics.

---

175   See http://www.onnuri.org/missions/2000-mission-ministry/.

176   The most current English publication about the M Mission is the aforementioned and forthcoming "Reverse Migration Ministries from Korea: A Case Study of Onnuri Community Church's M Mission." See also *Onnuri Community Church: The First 30 Years*, 272-276.

177   *Onnuri Community Church: The First 30 Years*, 272.

OCC's Approach

Beginning with Senior Pastor Lee Jae-hoon, as well as including OCC's various mission pastors, elders, program leaders, and consultants, OCC is proactively addressing this challenge of constructively integrating "'missional' and 'missions'" matters. Stated more in line with OCC's primary mission traits, the Holy Spirit is guiding *OnnuriCC* in its ongoing efforts to live out its inherent missional character, and its inherent "megachurch" character, to foster revival throughout the whole world.

In meeting this challenge, OCC has inherited what are largely alien, imported tensions associated with social-evangelistic ministries, modern missionary-sending methods and structures, and the Newbigen-inspired "missional church" discussions (as well as characterizations of "megachurches"). For his vitally important role, Pastor Lee is gratefully building on the Spirit's work through Pastor Ha; and, "anchored" in OCC's, Spirit-led "free and creative development" process, Pastor Lee is hoisting, I believe, a sixth "sail" that appropriates "missional church" themes. The particularly new aspect of this sixth sail – tailored to OCC members and programs – is implicit in the new vision phrase, "Fools for Christ."

Pastor Lee has suggested[178] that Onnuri Community Church might better consider itself as Onnuri *Commmunitas* Church. Doing so would stress the common experience and intimacy among OCC even as members humbly intermingle with others, rather than demarcating OCC off from others by emphasizing its own name, programs, and structures.[179] Pastor Lee exemplifies this humble intermingling by having taken on the role of an associate pastor of a small Methodist Church in Seoul that is involved with ministry to homeless people. Pastor Lee is also educating OCC about this theme through publicizing CGNTV's recent full-length movie-documentary about a German-American missionary in southern Korea, Elisabeth J. Shepping, who took on the Korean name "Seo Seo-pyeong,"[180] the movie's title.[181] Shepping's humble service among lepers, Bible teaching, fractured family background, and humble service embodied the kind of "Fool for Christ" life that Pastor Lee commends to OCC members.

---

178   He has done this in a few public messages during my times in Seoul.
179   This is my interpretation of his intended meaning.
180   Kim Jin-hyun, "Nurse Seo Seo-pyeong" *The Korea Times*, January 27, 2015, available online at http://www.koreatimes.co.kr/www/news/opinon/2015/01/162_172522.html.
181   See https://shepping.modoo.at/?link=q2i34p4r.

A whole additional area of focus for OCC mission, worth noting here as demonstrations of OCC initiative and creative ingenuity, is China and Chinese people. This area is in addition to OCC's multifaceted Japan focus described earlier, through Vision Churches, Love Sonata, a long-time Japanese worship service in Seoul (Seobinggo), and CGNTV. In its China focus, OCC holds regular "Vitamin-C" gatherings at its Acts 29 Vision Village to which Chinese house church leaders travel for training and encouragement. OCC, particularly through its KNCC-affiliated *Tonghap* connection, is also able to relate to registered Three-Self Chinese Church entities, including through sharing leadership training and discipleship program materials. OCC also has regular Chinese worship services, and recently it hosted the opening of a new initiative called "Mission China Diaspora." OCC also plans to construct a China Mission Center on Jeju Island, south of the Korean mainland. Through all these ways and more, OCC partners with various entities in seeking gospel progress among, and mission usefulness by, Chinese people within China and throughout the Chinese diaspora.

These creative OCC initiatives under Pastor Lee's leadership evidence the Spirit's work in guiding OCC in its particular "missional-missions" service. This study has highlighted the Spirit's foundational role in OCC's mission orientation by noting Pastor Ha's charismatic experiences, OCC's dramatic revival-fueled growth and ministries, and how OCC's mission vision has progressed. Two other evidences mentioned earlier are monumental for the Spirit's ongoing presence and work. One is the smooth pastoral succession from Pastor Ha to Pastor Lee starting in 2011. Another is the humble, collaborative leadership style that Pastor Lee exhibits in contrast to autocratic tendencies in other similar situations.[182] It may be the case that not all questions about OCC's mission orientation raised in this study and in others' minds will be answered (or even answerable) in familiar English-language categories, be they "'missional'-'missions'," "missional megachurch," "modality-sodality," or others. What is most important to recognize is the Spirit's presence and work as OCC continues to work out its mission orientation and emphases.

Next Steps

Pastor Lee Jae-hoon is well-studied in many areas, including in this "'missional' and 'missions'" area currently under discussion. Lee's scholarship,

---

182   Kim, Sung-Gun, 2015, 135.

astuteness, and spirituality will continue to serve well as he and OCC mission leaders continue to set budgets, allocate personnel, and discuss missiological topics. Their main assurance is from their experience of the Spirit of God's work throughout the formative Pastor Ha era. During that exhilarating quarter century, God shaped OCC's mission orientation and led its various efforts.

OCC's "Word and Spirit" foundation will also continue to serve it well. No human being can know how the Spirit will lead OCC in its upcoming understandings and practices of mission, including how it will take "missional missions" initiatives. What fresh insights and mission visions the Spirit will give through Pastor Lee remains to be seen. He and others are building on the Pentecostal-type of "This is that!" realizations of Pastor Ha. The movement-turned-"megachurch" labeled *Onnuri* Community Church took on a "missions" vision of sending out an astounding number of missionaries, then an even more expansive Acts 29 vision has led into the current, "missional" vision phase of "Fools for Christ." OCC's "anchor" of Spirit-instilled "free and creative development" will continue to hold steady, meaning that change will continue to be a normal part of OCC's life.

With respect to incorporating "missional church" themes into its mission orientation, as noted earlier those discussions in Korea have been fraught with linguistic and other imported stumbling blocks. Rather than focusing on the more narrow and contextually shaped features of the "missional church" discussion, OCC's stepping back and taking a more general approach of "missional theology," that "seeks to build the bridge between Biblical revelation and human contexts.... between orthodoxy and orthopraxy – between truth, love, and obedience,"[183] could prove helpful. The Spirit's guidance through the Scriptures in OCC's Korean setting – as well as OCC missionaries', mission ministries, and Vision Churches' varied international settings – will enable OCC's mission orientation to bring together theology and practice in answering the missiological questions it will continue to face. The Spirit will also guide OCC in shaping what those missiological questions are, instead of dealing with expatriates' or other imported questions that might not fit well in OCC's context.

Another area concerning which the entire OCC leadership would do well to take extra care is its posture toward its context(s). Churches and Christian

---

183   Tite Tienou and Paul G. Hiebert, "Missional Theology" *Global Missiology English*, Vol. 3, No. 2, 2005, 6, available online at http://ojs.globalmissiology.org/index.php/english/article/view/79.

movements tend to assume a posture somewhere on a spectrum having three points: universal-irrelevant, prophetically engaged, or particular-syncretistic.[184] That is, any entity like OCC could be "Christian" in name but disconnected to surrounding people's needs and concerns; or, OCC could be (and I believe is, at least in large part) responsive to, and participating in, God's work among its context; or, OCC could become frozen in its experience of blessings, fail to adjust to changing circumstances, and slip into simply reflecting and defending its bygone context. All groups get pulled toward either unhealthy side of the spectrum, and OCC is and will not be exempt from those pulls. Especially given OCC's strong Korean identity, coupled with its deep gratitude for God's granting revival to OCC so powerfully, slipping into preserving established forms of worship, dress, and programmatic patterns is a caution to which OCC's leaders need to remain alert. In mission outreach, unwittingly imposing its own materials and experiences onto others is a syncretistic temptation that OCC mission leaders are to resist in the name of encouraging God's people in different contexts to be prophetically engaged themselves with their own settings.

As much as anything, my hope is that the Spirit's work of testifying to Jesus Christ (John 15:26) will even increasingly fix Pastor Lee's and OCC's eyes on the triune God and the full panoply of divine mission initiatives throughout the earth and across the generations. A fundamental component of being "fools for Christ" is focusing on "Christ," not primarily on what it means to be "fools." Being enamored with God the Father, Son, and Holy Spirit and the *missio Dei* leads to "foolish" obedience in our various contexts of mission service. A theocentric focus also cultivates laboring for God's Kingdom instead of an OCC kingdom. As the Spirit continues to lead OCC the Korean megachurch, may God be OCC's primary focus and preoccupation.

*Epilogue -*온누리 *Onnuri* 大地

---

184   I have adapted these three categories from Lamin Sanneh, *Translating the Message: The Missionary Impact on Culture*. Revised and Expanded Edition. American Society of Missiology Series, No. 42. Maryknoll, New York: Orbis Books, 2009, 13-55.

As shown in this nuanced and multifaceted study of OCC's mission orientation, OCC is indeed a "big tent" of historical backgrounds, particular traits, and – within God's orchestration of his worldwide mission – Korean in character. OCC has faced various forms of opposition in its mission efforts, and it has faced the particular challenges of being a "missional megachurch" that conducts "missions" in "missional" ways. The Spirit's work has been palpable. I anticipate that OCC will continue to be one of the most mission-oriented churches that I and many others know.

Pastor Lee Jae-hoon and OCC's other mission leaders will continue to face opposition and nuanced missiological challenges. The Spirit of God's ongoing work means OCC's eyes are to be turned on the splendor of the Triune God and the magnitude of the *missio Dei*. The Spirit's work also means that OCC's mission vision is to acknowledge divine presence and work among those to whom OCC ministers the Good News of Jesus, as well as God's active use of other churches and organizations quite apart from OCC (but with some of whom OCC will partner). While *Onnuri Community Church* has an engrained posture of envisioning God granting revival to the whole world through its own particular zealous and varied efforts, the Spirit of God will continue to work throughout the earth and across all generations, using OCC and the multitude of other parts of the wider Body of Christ.

God has used OCC to break much new missiological and ecclesiastical ground. Labels and categories familiar to many of us English speakers – e.g., "Presbyterian," "Charismatic," "Pentecostal," "missions," "missional," "megachurch" – may not fit precisely as adequate descriptions of 온누리 *Communitas* and its manifold 선교와 사역. The God of all peoples, of the *onnuri*, knows all. The Spirit has worked in and through OCC. May he graciously continue to do so.

CCDA's Contribution to Urban Missiology

Joyce del Rosario

DOI: 10.7252/Paper. 000077

Abstract:

The Christian Community Development Association is one of the largest associations of urban church and parachurch ministries in the United States. Founded by John Perkins and Wayne Gordon, this association has been largely built around practitioners seeking racial reconciliation in their communities. In addition, CCDA has sought to develop the poor and marginalized by operating under eight principles: Relocation, Reconciliation, Redistribution, Leadership Development, Listening to the Community, Church-Based, (W)holistic, and Empowerment. These principles have set the framework for how many missionaries have entered into urban communities around the United States. With the increasing urbanization on a global scale, this panel will discuss CCDA principles and the need for CCDA practitioners and urban missiologists to work together.

One of the most heartbreaking aspects of my job was having to ask a young woman and her children to move out of the house. Leslie[1] was one such young woman. She had been in and out of the home three times which was the maximum allowed according to our policies. I let her live at the house a fourth time on the condition that she stay marijuana free. A few months later I had to ask her to leave after she tested positive for marijuana use. A few months after that, her landlord broke into the garage space she was renting with her two children and raped her.

While I'm not sure if letting her stay with us at New Creation Home would have ultimately prevented the situation, I had to take a hard stop and ask myself, "What are the bigger issues happening beyond our policies and programs?"

New Creation Home Ministries (NCHM) houses pregnant and parenting teenage mothers ages 13-22 and their children. NCHM has two residential homes and hosts a community-wide parenting class and Bible study for the young mothers in the neighborhood. The families at NCHM are homeless or housing-insecure, so the residents are a transient population. For every one step they took forward toward independence, they would often be pushed two or three steps back in a moment of crisis. Crisis seemed to dictate their every move.

As a practitioner, someone deeply entrenched in the day-to-day emergencies of the girls we served, I had little time to look at our missiological approach to teen moms. I took the model given to me, a model that was developed out of the needs and response of the community from, might I add, a person outside of the community. But after several incidents like Leslie's, I needed to find answers (or at least better questions) around the systemic injustices and relentless difficulty the young single moms faced.

After serving 15 years in full time urban youth ministry, it was time for me to return back to academia. My staff and I spent each day putting out one proverbial fire after another. It was a ministry of emergencies and we had little time to reflect on our model. At best, we could evaluate the existing programs, but that didn't answer the revolving door of young mothers in crisis. Part of my leaving the field for academia was to take the opportunity to research and consider the larger

---

1   Name has been changed.

approaches of how we do ministries, particularly in urban settings, particularly to marginalized groups like teen moms.

Because of my limited capacity in an urgent driven ministry, I realized I needed more partners to not only survive, but to thrive. I needed to partner with churches to support us locally through finances, prayers, and volunteers. I needed ministry partners to share our resources with and to come around our girls like a caring village. In hindsight, I also needed academic partners to help me develop a missiological approach that considered not only the immediate needs of our families, but also their larger spiritual, sociological, and psychological needs. We need deeper critiques of ministries, not just evaluations of programs, in order to further strengthen existing ministries, as well as encourage creativity toward new forms of missiological approaches.

Practitioners and missiologists need to work together because our contexts are not static. Immigration and incarceration are just a few ways our urban contexts change the landscape. Therefore, our missiology must also keep up with these changing landscapes in order to help equip practitioners in the field.

> In part, missiology's goal is to become a "service station" along the way. If study does not lead to participation, whether at home or abroad, missiology has lost her humble calling … Any good missiology is also a *missiologia viatoraum* —"pilgrim missiology." (Verkuyl 1978: 6, 18)

In other words, our missiology needs to hit the road somewhere. When I saw the theme of this conference; the dialogue between academia and practitioners I immediately thought of my connection with CCDA. The Christian Community Development Association offers that rubber and road connection to urban missiology. CCDA offers a network of urban ministry practitioners, who intimately know the needs of their neighbors in low-income, urban North America.

While little has been written about CCDA ministries in missiology publications, the dialogue between CCD practitioners and missiologists could create a mutually beneficial dialogue that strengthens both arenas. As missiologists, we need to build relationships with practitioners such as the ones in CCDA to help inform and shape our theories. In turn, the practitioners of CCDA also need relationships with missiologists to help evaluate how urban missions is being done, and whether or not their praxis needs a theological or missiological tune up, to borrow Verkuyl's service station analogy.

To clarify, I am not discussing missiologists and practitioners as if they are two different people. For example, Jude Tiersma Watson has proven one can live out both fields simultaneously and do it very well. Rather, I am discussing them as two different modes of operation. When I was in the field, I had little time to reflect and research, and now that I am in academia, I have very limited time to serve in the field. One can do both, but praxis and theory are centered and occupied in very different ways.

Today's presentation is an introduction for some of you, to CCDA so I will share a little of its history and founding principles as a way to encourage building partnerships and creating dialogue with more CCD ministries.

As one of the largest communities in urban North American ministry today, the Christian Community Development Association (CCDA) hosts over 3,000 people at their annual, national conference. The association is made up of hundreds of churches and para-church ministries from rural and urban settings.

While Harvie Conn and Manuel Ortiz established academic practices of urban missiology, John Perkins and the founding board members were gathering urban practitioners from around the country to meet, refresh, and equip for the important work of developing communities in a holistic manner. CCDA formally began at a meeting at the Chicago O'Hare airport, but the story truly began with two men by the name of John Perkins and Wayne Gordon.

John Perkins grew up in the 1930's and 1940's in rural Mississippi (Perkins and Gordon 2013: 16). Early on, he intuitively recognized the need for redistribution of economic wealth and power. "Redistribution" would later become one of the first of three R's that established the CCDA philosophy. The second R developed when his brother Clyde, who had come back from World War II, died at the hands of a white police officer. It was in the midst of his anger and hate that the seeds for CCDA were planted. Perkins committed to what would later be another component to Christian Community Development; reconciliation.

Soon after, Perkins moved to California where he developed relationships with Christian businessmen. Through those relationships he got involved in bible studies, prison ministries, and missions. In time, he began to feel the call back to his community in rural Mississippi. Another key component to CCDA formed because of this; relocation.

Wayne Gordon would hear John Perkins speaking while Gordon was a student at Wheaton College in the 1970's. Deeply impacted by Tom Skinner's book *Black and Free*, Gordon felt a call to serving the African American community. While at Wheaton, Gordon ministered in what was then called the "inner city" of Chicago in African American neighborhoods (2013: 24).

Gordon went on to live, teach, and coach in the North Lawndale community of Chicago. It was at the high school where he earned the nickname "Coach" as he is still called today. His initial desire was to teach bible studies to high school kids, but that ministry became a church and the church became a community corporation, complete with legal and medical services, a recovery program, and a gym just to name a few. To visit Lawndale today, one will find blocks of buildings owned by the Lawndale Christian Corporation. The church's presence and impact through the non-profit arm is not only evident in its physical presence, but also in the faces of the people they serve. The impact of Coach's almost 40-year ministry in the neighborhood is undeniable.

Gordon's advisory board consisted of John Perkins, Dolphus Weary, Tom Skinner, Bill Leslie, Mel Banks, and Ray Bakke. The advisory board meetings would soon become mini conferences at their Lawndale site in Chicago. Just a few years before these mini-conferences, Perkins was also establishing a network of his own in Jackson, Mississippi.

At the urging of his board, Perkins began to form a national network of urban ministers whom he had connected with through his speaking opportunities. They started the Jubilee Conference in Jackson, Mississippi, which would later become the template for the CCDA conference (2013: 28). The natural connections of urban practitioners at these conferences gave people the encouragement and equipping they needed, and soon a larger network would be formalized. In 1989, a gathering of fifty urban ministry leaders, both men and women, met at the O'Hare airport, to officially form the Christian Community Development Association.

John Perkins became the board chair and Wayne Gordon would soon become the President of CCDA.

One of CCDA's greatest contributions to urban missiology as well as to urban practitioners, is the philosophy of CCDA, explained by the eight key components. This philosophy of urban ministry continues to form and shape urban ministries across the US today, as well as other cities around the world. Because of the constraints of time, I will limit my description to the three principles, first developed by John Perkins.

Redistribution is the one of the first principles. Not to be mistaken for the idea of economic socialism, CCDA bases its understanding of redistribution on Psalm 24, that all is the Lord's. Redistribution should be an act of loving our neighbors by sharing, rather than a government function. In addition, redistribution is an act of social justice that goes beyond sharing money, but also advocating for justice in prison systems, housing policies, and education.

Under this key component, missiologists have an opportunity to bring theological and sociological research and reflection that can inform and undergird the redistribution efforts of practitioners.

Reconciliation is the next principle. CCDA focuses on reconciliation in three parts: people with God, people with people, and people groups with people groups (2013: 62). CCDA's commitment to reconciliation begins with recognition that there is a race problem, inclusive of the abuse and mistreatment of Native Americans and Africans brought to North America as slaves. "The goal of reconciliation is not to persuade or be persuaded, but rather to understand and to be understood and respected... Reconciliation is impossible without a willingness to request forgiveness and to forgive." (2013: 67) While this was a much-needed conversation over the past forty years and beyond, today there is question as to whether or not "reconciliation" has enough teeth to repair the damages around racial injustice in the United States. For example, Jennifer Harvey, author of *Dear White Christians: For those Still Longing for Racial Reconciliation* (2014), argues that a paradigm of reparations is needed before we can fully consider a paradigm of reconciliation. Reconciliation assumes that both parties have equal power and equal stake in asking for and giving forgiveness.

The third key component is relocation. "The concept of relocation is best understood in terms of what [CCDA] call a 'theology of presence' – a theology that lies at the heart of God's relationship with humanity." (2013: 46) This component is of particular interest in missiology as it gives different language for the sending of God's people by differentiating between relocators, returners, and remainers. "'Relocators' refer to people who are not indigenous to the community; 'returners' and 'remainers' by contrast, are indigenous residents. "(2013: 48) The terms returner and remainer help describe urban missionaries like myself who grew up in the immigrant communities of South Seattle (as David Leong has researched), left for education, and then returned to similar low-income communities with a call to serve the people with whom I most identify.

The important aspect of relocation is that the person becomes a part of the community they wish to serve. They have a vested interest in the well-being of their neighbors. CCDA encourages a theology of place under this principle. Hunter Farrell, in his keynote asked us, "Can missiology re-engineer itself? Can we pivot?" Working closely with CCDA practitioners is what will help us make the necessary pivot in urban missiology today.

Missiologists have the opportunity to tie together public missiology, ethics, and praxis in a cross-disciplinary way. Missiologists are positioned well to bridge the necessary (but still abstract) academic thought to the practical, yet limited capacities of practitioners. The partnership of a missiologist who brings theological and sociological research into urban ministries is one that exemplifies the Body of Christ in action.

Practioners can't live in the urgent all the time, but academics can't live in theory all the time as well. We need to do a better job with partnering with our local practitioners. One practical way we can accomplish this is to offer theological training to our local urban practitioners. We can offer training and insight to their staff and volunteers.

For example, as a doctoral student, I haven't had the bandwidth to be as directly involved in urban youth ministry as I have in the past, but I was able to volunteer with my friends at YouthFirst in South Central LA, to help train their part-time staff. This has not only added to their training resources without increasing their budget and therefore fundraising efforts, but it also keeps me grounded in terms of what I am studying and researching in academia.

When I volunteer with YouthFirst leaders, my interlocutors are not just Harvie Conn and Roger Greenway, but Twuance, Chayanne, and JayJay who are at the middle schools and high schools every day. They know what's going on in Inglewood and Westchester. They are the ones who help me shape and test my missiological theories. They are the ones who ask and inspire the pressing questions.

CCDA offers missiologists an escape from ivory tower naval gazing. I know that may sound heavy handed, but this is coming from my life as a practitioner from 2000 to 2015 when I needed resources to share with my board and staff. The only books that I could find that could help our context were from CCDA practitioners. CCDA practitioners are publishing books for fellow practitioners, but if I can be candid, they can be theologically and missiologically thin because that's not their starting place for reflection.

There is a dearth of urban missiological writing relevant to the urban context today. My esteemed panelists aside, we need more David Leong's and Daniel Hodge's and dare I say Joyce del Rosario's. CCDA offers us as urban missiologists a place to ask the bigger questions with practitioners and create with them innovative models for mission. CCDA offers missiologists essential interlocutors in the arena of urban missions. Whether it's around issues of short-term missions or gentrifying the hood in the name of Jesus, we need to be in dialogue with one another as partners in the mission to critically think about the implications of such practices.

Furthermore, we need greater missiological agility to keep up with practitioners who have been advocating, counseling, and ministering to people who have been directly impacted by executive orders, appointments, and acquittals that regardless of where you land politically, still has a deep and painful impact on immigrants and people of color in our cities today.

At the end of the day, it's not about creating a new model of communication theory based on the sociological findings of grounded theory research. It's also not about ministry models that operate in isolation, answering to urgent needs with little time for deeper self-reflection. It's about the Leslie's in our cities. It's about how to walk in the pain and the mess with young women like Leslie. It's about surrounding the Leslie's in our cities with a village of people contributing their resources and expertise in partnership with one another.

I mis-titled this panel and presentation a little. I still think, CCDA has contributed to urban missiology, but both have operated generally apart from each other. A better title would have been the needed dialogue between CCDA and Urban Missiology. There is a dearth in urban missiological writing and connecting with CCDA practioners, better yet, working alongside of them will help us reflect, create, and innovate models of mission that address the present and urgent issues for the urban landscape today.

Works Cited

Harvey, Jennifer.
>   2014.   *Dear White Christians: For those Still Longing for Racial Reconciliation.* Grand Rapids, MI: Eerdmans.

Perkins, John and Wayne Gordon.
>   2013.   *Making Neighbors Whole: A Handbook for Christian Community Development.* Downers Grove, IL: IVP Books.

Verkuyl, Johannes.
>   1978.   *Contemporary Missiology: An Introduction.* Grand Rapids, MI: Eerdmans.

Mission in Context

Empowerment for God's Mission Together Panel Presentation at American Society of Missiology

CLIFTON KIRKPATRICK
LOUISVILLE PRESBYTERIAN THEOLOGICAL SEMINARY

DOI: 10.7252/Paper. 000079

Buenos dias y muchas gracias! Good day and many thanks!

The four of us have been enriched by the opportunity to share together in a unique venture of offering a course for students and faculty – from Cuba and the U.S.A. – on Mission in Context during the January term of 2017. We are eager to share our learnings from this event with you and to get your feedback as all of us seek to engage in missional formation for the 21st century.

Any of you who have had the opportunity to visit Cuba are well aware of the incredible beauty and hospitality we find there, and that was certainly the case for the twenty students from Louisville Seminary who joined a similar group from Seminario Evangelico de Teologia in Cuba in January. Therefore, let me begin our presentation by sharing with you a short video produced by Grace Hellweg, one of our students, that will introduce you to this context of hospitality that we experienced.

[video at https://www.dropbox.com/s/fid7zpp6dxmcyyt/CubaMissionInContext.MOV?dl=0]

Before we get into the substantive issues we want to discuss with you, let me also do two other things to introduce you to this experience:

1. Introduce my colleagues on the panel and the themes they will address, and
2. Introduce you to the course schedule that we followed in Cuba.

I am pleased to introduce to you three friends and colleagues who provided leadership for the course and who will lead our conversations and reflections today:

- Dr. Ofelia Ortega Saurez, Professor and President Emeritus of the seminary in Cuba and President for Latin America of the World Council of Churches, will lead us in a reflection on *Together Towards Life*, the new mission statement of the World Council of Churches, and its relevance for mission today.
- Rev. Juan Sarmiento, a Doctor of Ministry student at Louisville Seminary and Associate Director for Mission at the Outreach Foundation, will lead our reflections growing out of the course on intercultural contributions to mission education, and

- Dr. Jo Ella Holman, Regional Liaison for the Caribbean for the Presbyterian Church (USA), will share with us issues related to contextual and pedagogical design.

I am Cliff Kirkpatrick, Professor of World Christianity and Ecumenical Studies at Louisville Seminary, and I will be introducing our biblical, missiological, and pedagogical foundations for our course and guiding our discussions today.

Let me begin by sharing how we spent our week together in Cuba[1]. While we sometimes veered a bit off from this schedule, it does show how we addressed these themes. We began our first day with a devotional and a study of biblical foundations for mission. We then moved to issues of context (which have often been issues of conquest related to Cuba). We closed our day introducing one another to the interfaith reality in Cuba and the USA. The second day we did further work on biblical and missiological foundations, then headed out to Matanzas to visit the museum on human slavery, to be in conversation with a Santeria community, and to engage in a dialogue between our two seminaries. For the balance of our time we each led in chapel, we shared mission experiences in the USA and Cuba, we visited a demonstration farm run by the churches, and we mainly spent time learning from one another in small groups. We concluded our time together by seeking to construct a missiology for faithful mission in context in Cuba and the USA – and with a fiesta.

The course was enhanced by the diversity (yet deep unity) among our group, by the context of two dramatically changing societies that have often been – and continue to be – at odds with one another, and by the powerful experiences of community we found with one another.

We also had students do reading before we arrived around our themes (and by and large they did) and agreed that the only texts we would use would be texts available in both Spanish and English. We also had excellent translators that gave us the ability to communicate with one another even when we did not speak both languages.

In my closing remarks, I want to share with you several perspectives and foundations that we took to the course, and we believe that these have been critical for giving our students the skills to do mission in context.

---

1   See appendix, "Course Schedule: Mission in Context (Jan. 16-20, 2017)."

There were five perspectives which we believe were foundational to making this course effective:

1. A critical pedagogy building off of the pioneering work of Paulo Freire that seeks to empower participants as active agents of God's justice.

2. An ecumenical perspective that builds on recent mission statements from the World Council of Churches (Together Towards Life), the Roman Catholic Church (The Joy of the Gospel), and the Lausanne Movement (The Cape Town Commitment).

3. A theological context from Latin America enriched by the biblical vision of Integral Mission and the deep spiritual resources of faith, worship, and joy.

4. A course whose primary context was the streets, the farms, the prisons to see God at work in Cuba, in the USA, and in the world.

5. An understanding of interreligious dialogue as a reality of critical importance in the practice of mission.

These perspectives, worked out in smaller and larger groups, enabled students to appreciate the marvelously diverse world in which God has called us to minister and empowers a new generation with the passion first articulated by Emil Bruner that "Mission is to the Church as fire is to burning."[2]

In relation to the bible, we started in the same place as the New Testament Church. Like the New Testament Church, we encouraged our students to be guided by the bible as a missionary document, written for a people engaged in mission in a new context. Drawing from the work of David Bosch in *Transforming Mission*[3] we encouraged our students to develop a missiology shaped by a theology of mission that assumes that the church is missionary by its very nature and that it is not so much that God's Church has a mission but that God's mission has a Church. We reminded them that the early church was composed of a radically multicultural community reflecting the diversity of God's love, and that it was engaged in a strange new context of empire, oppression, philosophical diversity, and a secular

2   Emil Brunner quoted in John Buchanan, *Being Church, Becoming Community.* Louisville: John Knox Press, 1996, p. 29.

3   David J. Bosch, *Transforming Mission: Paradigm Shifts in the Theology of Mission.* Maryknoll, NY: Orbis Press, 2011.

globalization, and.........was active in announcing that the reign of God is at hand and that it is "good news."

Through this course in Mission in Context, we sought to make those connections to the New Testament Church and to follow its example as we have been brought together as a multicultural community of students and faculty from Cuba and the U.S.A. guided by the bible, shaped by a missional theology, and engaging a radically new context (for us) of empire, oppression, and globalization – all for the purpose of announcing the "good news" of the reign of God in our time.

Appendix - Course Schedule: Mission in Context (Jan. 16 - 20, 2017) draft 3

Louisville Presbyterian Theological Seminary and the Protestant Seminary of Theology (Matanzas)

	Monday / Lunes	Tuesday/ Martes	Wednesday/ Miérc.	Thursday/ Jueves	Friday/ Viernes
7:30	Breakfast (be on time!)	Breakfast	Breakfast	Breakfast	Breakfast
8:00					CHAPEL **(S.E.T.)**
8:30	Devotional **(Chuchi/ Chavela**—SET's liturgical team)	8:30 Bible study on Matthew – **Clifton Kirkpatrick**	Contexto actual y misiología 2:	Where are we? Where are we going? **Jo Ella**	Discussion on visits made previous day- **Clifton/Clara**
9:00	Bible study on misión- **David Córtes-Fuentes** (PCUSA mission co-worker teaching at SET)	(Historical changes in the understanding of mission, according to David Bosch in Transforming Mission)	Discurso del papa Francisco sobre misión y evangelización- **Carlos Emilio Ham**	"Integral Mission," René Padilla. Evaluate mission initiatives. How does the context influence?- **Ofelia Ortega**	Constructing a missiology for the transformation of mission in Cuba and in the U.S. (work in groups)
9:45		CHAPEL **(Cuban students lead)**	CHAPEL **(S.E.T.)**	CHAPEL **(US students lead)**	**Carlos Emilio / Jo Ella/Clifton**
10:15	PAUSA/BREAK	PAUSA	PAUSA	PAUSA	PAUSA
10:30	Share personal stories of mission encounters in small groups. - **Ofelia Ortega/Clara Ajo/Jo Ella Holman/Clifton Kirkpatrick**	10:30 Bible Study, Book of Acts-**Orestes Roca** 11:30 Present Context and Missiology I: *Together Towards Life* (WCC) – **Ofelia Ortega**	Criteria and theological bases of each document. Dynamics of power– **Clifton/ Ofelia**	Depart for the Kairos Center (Baptist Church, Matanzas) -emphasis on integral mission: arts and worship; community development; water projects	Continued
12:30	Lunch/Almuerzo (SET)	Lunch/ Almuerzo (SET)	Lunch/Almuerzo (SET)	Lunch/ Almuerzo (DEMARI)	Lunch/ Almuerzo (SET)

2:00	Complete group work. **2:45** From personal stories to regional stories: the Caribbean and the sermon of Montesinos; las Casas **Jo Ella**	Visit to the San Severino Castle/ Fort; Slavery Route of the Caribbean (a UNESCO Heritage Site) – **Clara L. Ajo**	LPTS group shares from their U.S. context about mission activities related to inter-faith, justice and evangelism.	Summary/ Evaluation of the course (written and discussion) -**Ofelia y Clifton**
3:00	Presentation of clips and commentary on the film, *The Mission* and relevance to the history of mission in Latin America – **Fco. Rodés**	Continued Prayer in the dungeons (**Chuchi/ Chavela**)	VIsit to the Diaconal Ecological Center (DEMARI) -emphasis on integral mission, ecology, agriculture, community development and spirituality	Devotional (Cuban and U.S. students together)
3:30	Work in groups, **Fco. Rodés**	Visit with a representative of an Afro-Cuban religion.– **Clara L. Ajo**	Visit to the Valentine Church (Matanzas Presbytery) and recreation time together	
4:00		Continued		4:00 LPTS group departs SET
6:30	Dinner/Cena SET	Dinner/Cena SET	Dinner/Cena SET	
7:00			Dinner/Cena SET	
NOCHE	7:30 Preparation for inter-religious/ interfaith visits, **Clara L. Ajo**	7:30 Information on the Seminary— gathering with other students and faculty	8:30 Ecumenical Worship, Week of Prayer for Christian Unity	Fiesta!! Aguas Vivas (music group, Living Waters)

El grupo LPTS: el sábado, 21 de enero, 9:30 AM a ISCRE para una introducción del trabajo interfé del Seminario

Importance of the Document "Together Towards Life" for Latin America and Cuba

OFELIA ORTEGA

DOI: 10.7252/Paper. 000078

The World Council of Churches (WCC) brings together 345 Protestant, Orthodox, Anglican, and other churches representing more than 560 million Christians in 110 countries and works cooperatively with the Roman Catholic Church.

Since the integration of the International Missionary Council (IMC) and WCC in New Delhi, 1961, there has been only one official WCC position on mission and evangelism under the leadership of Dr. Emilio Castro, from Latin America.

We would like to highlight the following distinctive perspectives on the document "Together Towards Life":

1. The new ecumenical affirmation focuses on the mission of the Holy Spirit (*Missio Spiritus*) as its theological framework within the Trinitarian understanding of mission (*Missio Dei*);
2. The statement affirms that the goal of mission is affirming life in all its fullness;
3. Creation and spirituality are the heart of mission. In this statement, God's mission is understood beyond anthropocentric goals. God's mission is not only for the salvation of humanity alone but includes the earth and the whole creation;
4. The new affirmation is an ecumenical conviction. Compared to the 1982 text, in addition to Protestant thinking about mission, Orthodox, Pentecostal, and Roman Catholic mission understandings are strongly reinforced. The new landscapes of world Christianity are highlighted with the concepts of mission from the margins, issues of migration, and economic globalization;

The new statement strongly affirms a renewed commitment to evangelism in humility and respect. Sharing the news of Jesus Christ is an ultimate concern of mission. The text examines how to communicate the gospel in an individualized, secularized, and materialized contemporary world.

As the Latin American biblical scholar, Néstor Míguez affirmed: 'Together Towards Life' (TTL) has given us, on a global scale, the primary message and hermeneutic for mission and evangelism for our time, God is for life, and not just survival, but the abundant fullness of life. It is a holistic reading of the good news of God in Christ Jesus."[1]

We would like to highlight some of the most important perspectives of the document "Together Towards Life" for Latin America and Cuba.

1. In this document, the proper best way of defining the *Missio Dei* is the triune God's enduring invitation to "cross frontiers," to "built bridges," resulting in the church participating responsibly in history, culture, in people's lives, and in the created world, in which God constantly dwells.

   This has been a very important commitment of the Latin American Churches during the last decades, to try to find peace, unity, and integration among our countries and people. The affirmation approved by CELAC (Community of Latin America and Caribbean States) in January 2014 in Havana, declaring that Latin America is a "Zone of Peace," and the dialogue for more than four years in Cuba to try to end the terrible war and deathly situation in Colombia is a sign of hope in the world today.

   For Cuba, suffering for more than 50 years the USA embargo, we were crossing frontiers and building bridges with the support and caring love of friends and churches here in the States and Canada and in many other countries and churches in the South, including not only Latin America and the Caribbean, but an incredible understanding of our situation from Africa and Asia. The millions of bibles that we are receiving today are coming mainly from the churches in South Korea. This is a vital part of the mission of the churches in Latin America, the Caribbean, and Cuba.

2. A very important key concept within the TTL document is "mission at the margins" of society. But, just where are those margins within the particular landscape that our pastors and

---

1   Néstor Míguez, "Missional Formation for Transforming Discipleship", paper presented in the 2nd WCC-CWME Consultation on Missional Formation: Together Towards Life: Implications for Mission Studies Curriculum, 10-15 Sept 2016, Matanzas, Cuba.

lay leaders serve? Moreover, what types of skills are needed by these church members and leaders to do the mission at these margins? We need to enter to analyze the pedagogical concept of mission today. This was central to our experience in the two seminars between the Evangelical Theological Seminary in Cuba and the Theological Seminary of the Presbyterian Church in Louisville, Kentucky.

We always remember the words of Toyohiko Kagawa on his interpretation of the parable of the prodigal son when he affirms that God is always running from the center to the periphery. For more than three decades, we were in Cuba a remnant church, very few people in the pews of our local congregations. Now, since the end of the eighties until the present year 2017, we have more than 3000 to 5000 house churches and the missionary extension is now along the entire island.

3. A sentence in section 58, pg. 12 of the document has attracted our attention: "Mission is not a project of church growth, but the church's project to be an incarnation of God's salvation in the world, do we have today incarnational mission models that inspired us? Recently we celebrate in Havana 30 years of work of the Martin Luther King Center associate to the Baptist Church Ebenezer". In 30 years of work, this church together with the Center transformed the community where they are situated with a program of popular education and a network of community leaders with deep social concerns and a living testimony of incarnational faith. Art, music, popular reading of the bible related to the experience and cultural contextual situation of the neighborhood produced the transformation.

Some years ago, the Cuban government approved pastors and lay leaders to officially visit prisons for spiritual support. A Baptist pastor, Francisco Rodés organized a movement of voluntary chaplains to respond to this mission call. Now, there are more than 300 Christian leaders (women and men) that receive adequate formation from joining the movement but it is a different kind of visit, not only for evangelistic purposes but to work in a very interesting pedagogical way for the change and transformation of the people in prison and for the reincorporation of many of them to the society. They are developing a complete different methodological approach. Recently, Francisco Rodés and other Christian leaders were called from the military services to receive gratitude for the radical changes that they achieved in the lives of the people in prison. These are models of incarnational mission.

4. Our definition of the *Missio Dei* must always be that God sends us out to the road into a road with two-way traffic. This is a mission that is not anthropocentric, but biocentric. It is important to emphasize the theology of creation because we have been much affected by a constant emphasis being placed on a theology of sin and redemption. Several communities in Africa, Asia, the Pacific, Latin America and the Caribbean have beautiful concepts that describe the good transforming life we are talking about, because many of these communities are still living from and in an understanding of good and transforming life for all living things, the Earth, and beyond. *Ubuntu* from Africa is an expression of human relations lived in the community and in harmony with the whole creation (African anthropology and world view lived in community); there is no separation between culture and religion. In this world view, everyday things are an experience of the sacred. *Sangsaeng* is an ancient concept of Asia, "of a sharing community and economy, which allows them to flourish together". In Latin America, *sumak kawsay* is a concept that comes out of the world view of the indigenous peoples in Latin America about creation. It is an expression and praxis originating from the Quechua language of the Andes. *Sumak* means "fullness" and *kawsay* "life;" altogether meaning "well-being," "good living" or "integral quality of life for all". *Sumak kawsay* is both, tradition and realization in a going project

pointing to a cosmic community. This community is built on the principles of diversity, reciprocity, solidarity, and equality. In regions other than Africa, Asia, and Latin America, there must be concepts equivalent to these, which need to be explored together.

5. The TTL document challenges us with the concept of "radical hospitality" (para. 47, p. 10) How could we practice it today with the present situation of migrants and refugees? Is this a mandate from God today for our nations and communities? Today, *Missio Dei* demands the call of hospitality. As Christians, how should we respond to God's grace and generosity? By opening ourselves to others, we can find God in a new way (Heb. 13:2). Our willingness to accept the other in their otherness is the mark of true hospitality. In recent documents of the Lutheran World Federation, there is a very significant change of the word "hospitality." The word that is used is *conviviality* which has a better meaning to interpret the art and practice of living together. Our faith in the Triune God, the God of diversity and unity, the God of Creation, who gives fulfillment, feeds and sustains us, helps us to be hospitable and open towards everybody. We have been given the generous hospitality of God's love. We cannot act differently.

6. God's Spirit can be found in all cultures that affirm life. We acknowledge that there is an inherent value and wisdom in diverse life-giving spiritualities. Therefore, authentic mission makes the other a partner in, not an object of the mission. Locally and globally, Christians must engage with people of other religions and cultures building societies of love, peace, and justice. The current religious pluralism, also called the interfaith context demands a dialogue of religions, not just to get doctrinal agreements or to establish a common form of worship, but to discover the plurality in which God is manifest in history, the plurality of ways of salvation, the plurality of humankind to these manifestations.

Our experiences in Cuba have been included in the program of Theological Education at the Evangelical Seminary of Theology in Matanzas, a course of Sciences of Religion in Havana, which at present has 120 students from various religions (there are 8 religions in Cuba and a Platform of Cuban Religions for Peace), as well as agnostic students and others with no religious affiliation of any kind. When Christian awareness is open to global awareness, a new type of sustainable theology can emerge. This new theology requires a new kind of theologian, men and women with a new type of multidimensional, transcultural, and trans-religious awareness.

7. The WCC document includes a very important aspect of the development of missiological trust for mission arising out of the local communities, and the need to recognize the wisdom of the local population. Local congregations are frontiers and primary agents of mission.

Evangelism is grounded in the life of the local church where worship (*Leiturgia*) is inextricably linked to witness (*Martyria*), service (*Diakonia*) and fellowship (*Koinonia*). (II Corinthians, chapters 8 and 9).

Recently in the most difficult economic time of my country Cuba (the so-called "special period" that began in the nineties), the National Association of Psychology organized a survey in Havana with the question; How can you survive in this difficult social and economic situation? They were surprised when the answer of many persons was the support, love, and hope of my local congregation.

These local spaces are the privileged place of actions of the *Missio Dei*. The TTL document included a pneumatological focus on Christian mission. We love this affirmation because in Cuba we believe in the subversive actions of the Holy Spirit that surprise us in incredible ways, opening doors for the churches in difficult situations, helping us to use imagination and creativity to renew our liturgies, and to develop new ways to do the mission and diaconal work of the churches for the well-being of Cuban society.

We agree with Néstor Míguez when he affirmed: "Coming to the present century, three major documents, representing different Christian traditions have brought again into considerations the centrality of mission for the theology and praxis of the Gospel faith. Together Towards Life (TTL) can be matched considering important differences and emphases, with the Pontifical Encyclical *Evangelii Gaudium* (EG), with the antecedent in the final document of the V CELAM meeting in Aparecida, Brazil, and the following Encyclical *Laudate Si* (LS)- and with the Cape Town Commitment (CTC) of the Lausanne Movement.[2]

<u>Some important convergences in these three documents:</u>

- Affirming life in all its fullness.
- Economy and economic practice are always a matter of faith as they touch the very core of God's will for creation.
- The need to proclaim Jesus the Messiah and the Reign of God.
- The joy of the Gospel gives life.
- Discipleship and evangelization are keywords for all three documents.
- A pneumatological focus on Christian mission.
- Unity prevails over conflict. Ecumenism is an indispensable path to evangelization.
- For the church, the option for the poor is primarily a theological category rather than a sociological one.
- The mission is at the center and purpose of Christian existence.
- The church in each context is called to serve (*Diakonia*).
- Interreligious dialogue is a necessary condition for peace in the world.
- A new missionary paradigm is emerging to respond to the new era in the world and a new time in civilization.

---

2   Ibid, Néstor Míguez, "Missional Formation for Transforming Discipleship," p. 2.

- Healing is also one of the Gifts of the Holy Spirit (1 Cor. 12:9, Acts 3). The mission should foster the full participation of people with disabilities and illnesses in the life of the church and society.
- The mission involves deconstructive patriarchal ideologies, upholding the right to self-determination for indigenous peoples, and challenging the social embeddings of racism and casteism.

The mission is holistic and integral, because the Triune God has a mission of grace in relation with humanity and that mission is holistic and universal in salvation, restoration, liberation, healing, compassion, reconciliation. God's reign is that of life, love, justice, and peace.

To bring this reflection to a close, we want to point out that perhaps this is not the worst epoch of humanity, but without a doubt, it's not the most brilliant. It is a time with its own difficulties, which are so particular they can't be resolved with simple answers or recipes drawn from the past. It is also, however, "our epoch," that in which we have been called upon to live because God willed it to be so, and in the midst of this epoch-not on the edges, but in the midst-is where we are summoned to share the good news and to act upon the words of the Gospel.

This prayer of Archbishop Arnulfo Romero, a Latin American martyr helps us to see that, "We are prophets and prophetesses of a future that is not our own."

We have to listen to the voice of God and the clamor of God's people.

We have to open our hearts to respond to those who suffer.

To speak prophetical language to respond to those who suffer.

The hands to work for the poor and the needy.

The mind to reflect on the good news of the Gospel.

The will to respond to God's call.

The spirit to wait for God in prayer, and to intercede for the church and the world.

Intercultural Contributions to Mission Education

JUAN J. SARMIENTO

DOI: 10.7252/Paper. 000076

The study of mission is a strong element in programs of study at both Seminario Evangelico de Teologia in Matanzas (SET) and the Louisville Presbyterian Theological Seminary (LPTS). Both institutions incorporate missiology, ecumenism, and global Christianity as significant areas of emphasis. That, in addition to the strong relationship between Presbyterians in Cuba and in the U.S. prepared the way for Jo-Ella Holman, Regional Liaison for the Caribbean with the Presbyterian Church (U.S.A), to begin conversations with both schools in 2013 about the possibility of a combined course characterized by intercultural and contextual approaches to teaching and learning for mission.[1]

The diverse participant composition of the course required significant changes in relation to the design of missiology courses. During the first course in 2015, 23 students made up the course, 13 from the US and 10 from Cuba.[2] The second iteration of the course in January 2017 had the participation of 32 students, 16 from the US and 16 from Cuba. Although the students have had similar levels of formal education,[3] the differences in their ecclesial and ministerial experiences - in addition to cultural and linguistic experiences- are quite significant.[4]

The course as part of recent trends in mission education

The careful attention given to intercultural dynamics in this course is reflective of similar efforts towards mission formation considering the growing demographic diversity in the United States and greater involvement of non-western Christians for witness and service beyond their own contexts. As Dan Aleshire has noted, "cultural" has gradually become a predominant term used by institutions in the U.S and Canada to designate the type of programs that had formerly had words like "missions," "mission," or "missiology," as part of their names. The table below

---

1 Holman, Jo Ella (2015) 'We Make the Road by Walking': An Intercultural and Contextual Approach to Teaching and Learning for Mission. In Miguel Alvarez (Ed.), *The Reshaping of Mission in Latin America* /Regnum Edinburgh Centenary Series. Volume 30 (p 221-234). Oxford, UK: Regnum Book International.

2 Holman, 227.

3 Except for a Doctor of Ministry student from the US seminary, all the others have been Master's degree students in their second or final year of study. Students from SET have been a combination of fifth-year, Licenciatura students and recently graduated students.

4 LPTS students have come from Presbyterian, United Methodist, Baptist and Pentecostal backgrounds while among SET students were Presbyterians, Baptists, Anglicans, Quakers and Seventh Day Adventists.

represents both the growth of those programs (from 22 to 61) and the changes in the nomenclature in recent years.[5]

	1995	2005	2015	Notes
"Missions…"	N= 22	N=42	N=61	Declines by almost half
"Cultural…"	64%	55%	31%	Increases significantly
"World/ Global"	27%	36%	46%	Slight increase
Other	5%	7%	10%	Increases

Similarly, the enrollment in Doctor of Missiology programs has significantly decreased during the same period.

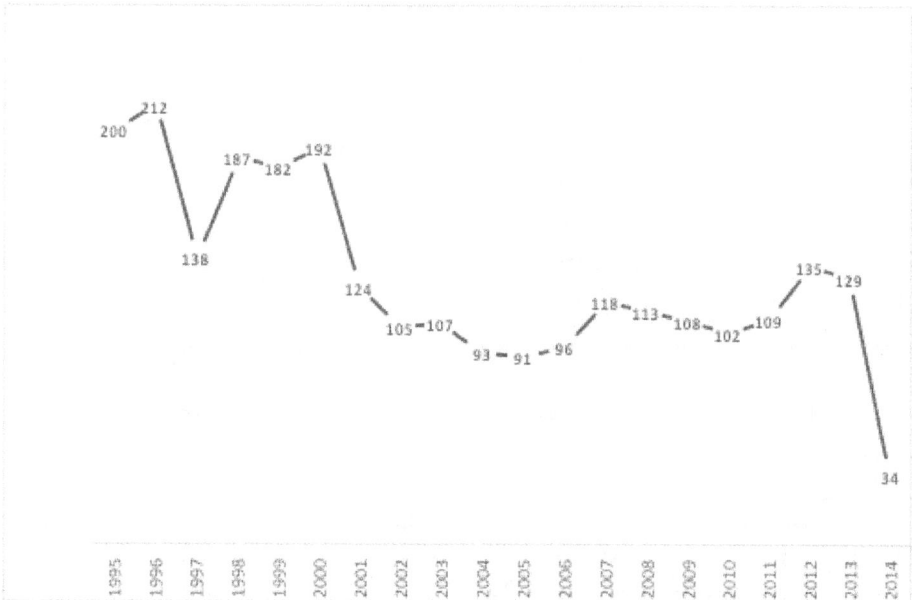

5   Dan Aleshire, executive director of the Association of Theological Schools in the Unites States and Canada (ATS) presented this data during the plenary address for the 2015 gathering of the Association of Professors of Mission entitled "Naming and Numbering Education for Missions: Changing Patterns Among ATS Member Schools". Although not previously published, he kindly forwarded it to me.

Intercultural realities of theological education

Anticipating the moment when the white population is projected to be less than 50 percent of the total and as a way of supporting and assisting schools to prepare for that, The Association of Theological Schools (ATS) has undertaken "Preparing for 2040: Enhancing Capacity to Educate and Minister in a Multicultural World."[6] To accomplish this, they are actively promoting the use of the Intercultural Development Inventory (IDI) among its member schools as a tool used to "build cultural competence" in schools and organizations in more than 40 countries in all continents.[7] Recent statistics released by the ATS indicate that in the last three decades the enrollment of students classified as other than Euromerican has increased from 10% to 41%.[8] The percentage of Latino students has doubled in the last 15 years and Asian enrollment currently represents 9 percent of the total. Along those lines, a recent campaign from Presbyterian World Mission called Training Leaders for Community Transformation, which promoted collaboration in leadership development efforts, identified inter-contextual concerns as a priority of most partnering programs in the 30 participant countries.[9]

Intercultural considerations in the course

Following a "team teaching" approach, the professors for the course display the interculturality that the course seeks to promote. Ofelia Ortega, Daniel Montoya Rosales, Clara Luz Ajo, and Carlos Emilio Ham have delivered lectures in Spanish from SET, while Clifton Kirkpatrick and Jo Ella Holman have done it in English. In addition, other faculty from both SET and staff colleagues from Louisville Seminary have been brought in to share with students in areas of their competence.

Holman describes the collaborative design process of the course "as one in which each side contributed ideas for readings and exploration."[10] The team

---

6   Edwards Armstrong, Janice (2009) CORE: An Evolving Initiative. *Theological Education*. Volume 45, Number 1. pp 71-76.

7   Intercultural Development Inventory (2017) Retrieved from https://idiinventory.com/.

8   Meinzer, Chris and Smith Brown, Eliza (2017 March) New data reveal stable enrollment but shifting trends at ATS member schools. Retrieved from http://www.ats.edu/uploads/resources/publications-presentations/colloquy-online/new-data-reveal-stable-enrollment.pdf. The percentage include international students.

9   Sarmiento, Juan. To the Ends of the Earth. *Mission Crossroads*. Spring 2016. P 4.

10   Holman, 227.

made sure that all the materials would not only be in both Spanish and English but several of their authors were from Latin America. Preparing for the five-day intensive experience of direct instruction and interaction played an important role in the course. In 2017, it included two days of orientation for the U.S. students co-facilitated by Dr. Carlos Emilio Ham, President of SET. In addition, a series of four sessions of Spanish conversation were offered to students in basic and intermediate levels of proficiency.

Communication during the gathering in Cuba was facilitated by professionally trained interpreters making use of excellent equipment provided to that end. A look at the evaluation forms for both the 2015 and the 2017 classes indicate that the intercultural, binational group of participants was an asset in their understanding of the practice (praxis) of mission. Here is a comment that illustrates the results:

In some ways our experience as a diverse group was an example of the concepts we talked about. We had to work hard at communicating, crossing boundaries, and being in real relationship. We did not get there completely, but we were enriched by each other's ideas and presence.

Other relevant responses in the evaluation can be summarized as follows:

Question	2015	2017
Did you feel that your perspective was heard?	21 "Yes" 1 "Sometimes, 1 "No"	28 "Yes" 1 no response 1 "As a white male I felt that I needed to hear the perspective of others"
Will you be able to use specific parts of the course that you will be able to use in your ministry in your local context?	23 "Yes"	30 "Yes"

Will you be able to use specific parts of the course in working with international partnerships or with people of other nationalities in your ministry?	22 "Yes" 1 "No"	29 "Yes" 1 "More or less"
If this course were offered again, would you recommend it to your friend	23 "Yes"	30 "Yes"

Students also indicated the most significant elements of the educational experience in the evaluations. In response to the question "What was your favorite part of this course?" the majority (53%) mentioned small groups, followed by site visits (31 %). In spite, or perhaps precisely because of the cultural differences, the time given to student interaction beyond the classroom seems to have provided the most enriching opportunities for students from both groups.